People are gross.

EXISTENTIAL THIRST TRAP

ESSAYS BY ROBERT DEAN

Existential Thirst Trap
Copyright © 2022 Robert Dean

All Rights Reserved

ISBN: 979-8-218-10269-2

Without limiting the rights under copyright reserved above, no part of this publication may be reproduced, stored in or introduced into a retrieval system, or transmitted, in any form, or by any means (electronic, mechanical, photocopying, recording, or otherwise), without the prior written permission of both the copyright owner and the above publisher of this book.

Cover by Matthew Revert

Edited by Claire Rudy Foster

Interior Formatting by Lori Michelle
www.TheAuthorsAlley.com

For Jackson and Luke,
the best two dudes to ever happen to me

TABLE OF CONTENTS

Part One: Free State 1
    Whiskey, Smoke, and Lies
    Good Time Charlie
    Grease & Grim
    Bathroom Code
    A Playlist will Never be a Mixtape
    What's Your Hustle?
    A Coffee Shop in Strange City
    New Orleans Hard
    Free State

Part Two: Rotten Heart 51
    Bare Soul
    Working Class Joe
    Plagued Mind
    Anxiety, My Ex-Wife, and Me
    Little Bastard
    Plan B
    One Gray Hair at a Time
    Personalized
    Some Disaster
    Kitchen Necromancy
    Last Course
    The Rotten Heart of Love

Part Three: Good Men and Gators 105
    Please, Don't Pass the Cake
    The Sound of Skateboard Wheels
    Old Dudes
    Dinosaur Skulls
    I Saw the Light
    What Else Should I Say?
    I Hope There Are Crocodiles in Heaven

"I did it."—Clark Griswold

PART ONE:
FREE STATE

WHISKEY, SMOKE, AND LIES

I have absolutely no pleasure in the stimulants in which I sometimes so madly indulge. It has not been in the pursuit of pleasure that I have periled life and reputation and reason. It has been the desperate attempt to escape from torturing memories, from a sense of insupportable loneliness and a dread of some strange impending doom.
— Edgar Allan Poe

ON BOURBON STREET, they pay you every Friday. They have to—the street is run by too many whiskey-swilling scumbag pirates. People come and go, and they've got bar tabs to pay for if they wanna be let back in some of those joints. Debts to settle. Otherwise, they risk getting got—just the culture.

Back before everyone had accounting software, all of these bars' front offices had an accountant who knew how to cook the books. To save a little bread on their end, they'd offer you a deal with the devil: all cash, all on a check, or half cash and half on a check. The half-cash option was the move because it allowed them to claim you but only as part-time. You still got taxes taken out and you got your money back. You can't do that shit today.

I always kept $60 to get wrecked with. It was the rule. After wandering the Quarter, I usually wound up on a barstool at the end of the Abbey's stick, down on Lower Decatur. Jameson and PBR, the usual pair of handcuffs.

ROBERT DEAN

One night, my friend Jenn was working the bar. She pointed to the old cat next to me.

"Oh shit, you gotta meet Bobby," she said. "He's a writer! Y'all should talk."

The man was a regular old sea dog. Collared shirt opened wide at the neck, a dark suit jacket despite the New Orleans humidity. The old-timer had seen action. He looked like warmed-over dog shit but was kind enough. He mumbled something at me about a name, but I couldn't make it out. I already had a few pours circulating in my system. Plus, I'm terrible at names. We got to talking, so I ordered a round of shots. Apparently, he'd worked for some magazines and was in the game for a long time. I'm a ho for the old school newshounds. Whenever I meet someone who's been on a beat or comes from newspapers, I'm all ears. Let me siphon the fucking brain out of your body.

"I just got one, you get the round," I said.

"No, motherfucker, you're the young cat. You buy, I'll get the next one. I got money, fucker. Pay your respects to your elders."

I bought us two tall whiskeys, and we got into books, writing, and my living in New Orleans. He didn't love the loud music in the Abbey but endured it because he liked the people he met. With a few exchanged chest pokes, cursing with every other word, we were dialed in, talking about ledes, how a story moved, how to not make certain mistakes.

By the time we downed a bottle or two of Jameson, he looked at me and clucked, "This is it, man. You're a real fuckin' writer. I don't know if you suck or not, but you gotta be out there in the shit, living life, kid. Most of these fake fucks ain't got it; you gotta be willing to die a little. You can't be a pussy. You gotta collect scars like baseball cards, make mistakes."

He jabbed at my flesh, "You think I didn't notice that tattoo? That son of a bitch was my best friend."

On my right arm, I have a big Ralph Steadman drawing

EXISTENTIAL THIRST TRAP

of Hunter S. Thompson from *Fear and Loathing in Las Vegas*. The old-timer pulled out his wallet—which put George Costanza's to shame with its sheer size—and whipped out one of those photos from the late 1970s with the rounded corners. It was a much-younger him and Hunter. There was also handwriting on the back, which was also clearly Thompson's.

This was where the night got sketchy and hazy. We drank *a lot* of booze. We sat at the edge of the bar, going shot for shot. We got into old school news guys, drank more. He kept wanting me to go to the bathroom to dog blow. This dude was *old*. He put down the drink like a professional. The guy had to be creeping seventy. We were deep on Bukowski, "a fat asshole with a big dick." We talked shop on Studs Terkel, who we both respected. We commiserated on Flannery O'Connor, "best of the Southern Gothics, got the shaft because she was a woman," and even stumbled into a little politics. He didn't love Obama but understood he was needed.

And he still kept trying to get me to do coke in the bathroom. An impossible feat. If we wanted to drag some snow, the Abbey bathrooms are the size of an upright coffin. Two people ain't fitting unless they're banging—very uncomfortably, with one foot in the toilet. After a while, my companion said he'd done work for *Rolling Stone* and was an editor at *Playboy*. He regaled me with stories from Woody Creek, told me that he was the guy Hunter based Doctor Gonzo on, said he and the lawyer, Oscar "Zeta" Acosta, were responsible for those stories. The Gonzo character was an amalgamation of both of them.

"When they shot Hunter out of the cannon and all that hullabaloo, I was there. Hunter didn't blow out his brains because he was sad. He had fucking cancer, man. He didn't want anyone to see him weak. He couldn't bear people knowing he wasn't the invincible legend, so he went out like his hero Hemingway. The fucking idiot."

ROBERT DEAN

How true this is, I can't tell you. I have no way to fact check this. This is what he told me. He talked the talk. My bullshit radar is fine-tuned—I can break anyone's timeline in seconds flat. I pay too much attention to the details of a story, and this cat knew interior facts about Thompson—stuff about their friendship and how he would edit his work, the kind of thing that I don't think anyone can just make up. But New Orleans tends to drag people out of the ether and make them real for a moment. If he was a bullshitter, the man was deadly in the arts. When I was seeing triple, it was time to head back to my shotgun house deep in the Treme. I thanked the mumbling stranger for his stories and the booze. He grabbed something out of his suit jacket and scribbled his name and number on it.

"Get a hold of me. I wanna see your writing. I wanna know if you're any good."

I tipped my White Sox cap and made the eleven-block stumble back to my place. I fell face-first into my couch, waking up the next afternoon with my Vans on my feet. I pulled my things out of my pockets methodically, like a surgeon prepping the table. That's how drunks keep track of their adventures. You gotta see what falls out. Sometimes it's a number, a bottlecap, or a switchblade. And there, written on the back of a burlesque flier, was a name and number that was wholly and utterly illegible. No one on earth could have deciphered that code.

Could I have gone back to the Abbey and asked around? Probably. I didn't bother. I got the stories. The guy knew his subjects, from Baudelaire to Jimmy Buffet. He sold it, one word at a time. He never found out I'm a shitty writer, anyhow. Many times, the lie is better than the truth.

GOOD TIME CHARLIE

YOU KNOW WHAT'S wild about brains? You'll be in the middle of the toothpaste aisle, grabbing a buy-one-get-one-free pack of Colgate, and a random memory will zap through your head in a split second, like you're some Vietnam war survivor. In a flash, you remember some dark shit you pushed way, way down there—the stuff where the spiders and skeletons dwell, those gross nights and ugly mornings. In the same mystic boogaloo, you recall laughing when you texted a friend six years ago about someone farting in the elevator with an old lady who told the offender to "go take a dump." Life is dark, it's stinky, and it's fucking weird.

I get random New Orleans flashbacks all the time. I'll be talking with someone about the city, and some kernel I haven't thought about in a decade will surge through my head, leaving me breathless and wondering how I've managed to dance so close to chaos for so long and still remain unscathed. Well, relatively unscathed.

Somewhere in the pre-Uber days, Preston, my best friend, and I had closed down working on Bourbon Street and hit the service industry dives for a few after-work sodas. When it was time to stumble home, we had to figure out how to get there. Back before you could swipe your finger on a smartphone screen, things were a little more complicated. The streetcar line was convenient because it cost $1.25 to ride one way, rounding the bend off Canal and heading north on St. Charles Avenue. The ride with stops took about twenty-five minutes but didn't start rolling till after 5 a.m. There was also the option of calling a cab, but in those days, the cabs were crazy expensive. You were lucky if they showed up at all. Typically, if you called a taxi, you'd have to wait at least twenty minutes for them to arrive—so why spend $40 to get home when we could wait it out and sober up waiting on the streetcar?

Standing on the corner of Canal and Carondelet, we were not in the world's prettiest company. We were waiting idle with tired cooks, other drunks, and a few lowlifes lost deep in the weeds looking for cheap transport just as we were. As the minutes passed, the eerie silence of the streets settled in. Late-night hustlers cruised past, looking us over—which is never a good feeling. More than once, scoundrels have gotten out of cars with their guns pointed at everyone, demanding their wallets and phones. That's also part of the gig when you're taking public transportation so late at night. As Preston chain-smoked, I could feel my kidneys start to float. I had to pee. And I didn't want to find a corner, somewhere hidden. God only knew what kind of villains would be lurking in the dark. As we loitered there, hoping the streetcar would magically appear, a guy in a beat-up late-90s Honda Civic rolled up.

"Aye, if anyone's going Uptown, I'll give you a ride. $10 each."

Preston and I looked at one another and went for it. Ten bucks to get home in ten minutes seemed like a good deal. The streets were looking extra bleak, like something could pop off. Unless this dude had a gun, we could take him in a fight. Were we getting in the car with a potential serial killer? Maybe? He didn't look the type, but they never do, so whatever. We rolled the dice.

Getting in the car, I made it very much known that we were two broke Bourbon workers, not bartenders (they tend to have cash from their shifts, so they're easy prey and

EXISTENTIAL THIRST TRAP

tend to get rolled). It turned out the driver was super friendly. He spent most of his nights giving people downtown rides to non-sketchy parts of the city. He was doing the Uber thing long before the start-up existed, and at $10 a ride in a small city, he made his gas money and then some. Could we have wound up in a shallow grave? It's possible, but we also got home a lot quicker, and boy, did I have to pee. That ten-dollar leak was one of the best of my life.

One of my other WTF moments—in bold, big-ass letters—was a long night after a bender at F&M's on Tchoupitoulas Street. It's a notorious sloppy college-drunkard fuck fest. It's pretty much the last call of the underage and over-served crowd. The hottest messes of the local colleges party HARD here. If you're a college kid and can't bang someone within a few hours of working this room, you need to go to one of those pimp schools they advertise on television. Sketchy older guys hang there on weekend nights, which is gross. Those dudes lay down the plastic to buy endless rounds of shots, aiming to wind up with an 18-year-old. Yikes. All I can say is: that's their trauma to decode, not mine.

At F&M's, the pool table's war-torn felt was covered in plywood. I guess after so many hammered girls dancing on it in heels, they gave up any notion of playing an actual game of billiards. Everything about this place was rancid. The bar was a museum of finger banging in filthy bathrooms, while a particular section should be noted for washing the vomit out of braces. Pass-outs, half-assed bar fights, metric tons of puke. Somehow, I ended up there.

Laws in New Orleans are more suggestions than hard and fast rules. Two attractive female friends told me they used to hang out at this bar. They made friends with the cops who cruised by regularly. One of them was celebrating a birthday—she was probably all of 22—so the cops let them jump in the squad car. They drove around flashing the lights, scaring people for fun. These cops let the girls wear their hats and everything.

I had just started working on Bourbon Street. A few friends of mine had put roots down in New Orleans for a few years; one of their comrades had made it off the street and into this hell hole. Matt, Devin, Justin, and I saddled up to the bar. Matt and Devin played in a death metal band together, while Justin had just returned from Iraq a few weeks before. He came home with a scorching case of PTSD. When the tequila went down, the ghosts of the past came out. All three of these guys grew up within the New Orleans area code or just next door over in Metairie. They knew the deal with this bar long before I did.

We proceeded to get scary drunk. Like, the kind of drunk where you open the front door of the bar, projectile vomit into the street, and still get served.

After a few hours of that, we wanted po boys. Everyone who's been on a bender knows at some point in the night, you want sex and grease. Considering that this was a weeknight and we were the only people in the joint, sex was out. We headed to the street, pulled our pants down around our ankles, and peed, screaming at one another, intoxicated.

We shouldn't have driven. I know this and am here to make a M.A.D.D. speech about the stupidity of driving drunk. I am sober enough as I write this, and I get it, okay? Logic would have said, "Let's take a cab. Let's walk. Let's hire a Sherpa to guide us via Pedicab." Something sane. However, we were crazy that night. We walked straight toward Devin's car. Three of us made it. Devin was behind the wheel. I rode shotgun because I'm tall as fuck. Matt was trying to figure out what to do with the beer he was holding in the back.

We were only missing Justin, who was lagging behind. He staggered along, yelling at us to hold up. He had to piss. As his wang fell out of his jeans and the urine started

EXISTENTIAL THIRST TRAP

flowing, we failed to see what exactly he was pissing *on*—a parked New Orleans police cruiser.

Within seconds, two doors opened, ejecting two very upset cops, both shouting *what the fuck*. Our car was parked a few yards away, so we couldn't hear the small talk—which should have resulted in Justin face down on the squad with a nightstick up his ass, but, you know, white privilege.

We heard him explain, "I'm a vet, man. I just got home from Iraq! This is one of my first nights going out."

This was a lie because this was certainly *not* one of our first nights out. The fuzz demanded identification, so Justin walked over to Devin's door, yanked it open, shoved his hand down into the side cubby, and pulled out his wallet. He held his wallet up with one hand for them to see. Then, to my horror, he yelled, "I got a gun too!" and pulled that out so they could see it too.

"Put the fucking gun back and come over here!" one of the cops said.

Justin put the gun back and slammed the door shut. The three of us were sweating bullets. For Devin, this was a clear DUI. For us, we were loaded—that's an easy public intoxication beef. Not to mention the gun.

Grabbing his wallet, the cops looked over Justin's info. Being a combat vet with accolades must have been notated somewhere in his information.

The cop looked over his info, folded the wallet, and through gritted teeth, offered: "Thanks for your service. Don't ever piss on my car again." He walked back to the cruiser without a word.

Justin, grinning like a hero, climbed into the back. We got our po boys, and then we absolutely did not go home and go to bed like good adults. Instead, we drank until the sun came up with Devin peeling out in front of my house, blasting Cannibal Corpse, waking up the neighborhood like a sadistic alarm clock. We're thoughtful people like that— blast beats, near-felonies, and cop cars covered in pee.

GREASE & GRIM

THIS ONE IS BAD. I had friends in town from Chicago. They flew down to New Orleans for the weekend, looking to get weird. They all worked at a tattoo shop, and the deal to join the party was you had to come with two thousand dollars cash. That was the buy-in. All of this money was to be blown on betting the black at Harrah's casino, luxurious meals, in the bars, and throwing dollars at strippers. That was the deal. No one was going home playing it safe—big tips, big bets, big hangovers.

They'd flown in the night before and spent Friday tossing dice on the craps table. Some of them came out ahead, while others were already down five bills or better. There were four of them, including one of my best friends, Bryan. When I got off dealing with the happy hour crowd at The Swamp, I met them over at the Dungeon. At the time, the Dungeon was a metal/punk hang out spot that snaked between two buildings with a little back nook where you could hide in plain sight. It basically looked like a *Hellraiser* movie where they served Coors.

The drinks were strong as high-powered gasoline, while beautiful girls worked behind the bar. The jukebox was packed with the hits, capturing everything: Social Distortion, Slayer, and Johnny Cash. For years, it was one of my go-to bars. I even had my name on a plaque right on the bartop, a memento for dedicated locals only.

After I'd gotten there and gotten introduced to the guys

EXISTENTIAL THIRST TRAP

I didn't know, we had a few drinks. All shift, I'd dealt with dancing around to Robin Thicke's "Blurred Lines" while enduring requests for worse songs. I needed a few minutes to enjoy a beer. After multiple shots, we'd had our fill of Johnny Cash's *American Recordings* material, along with a steady diet of Slipknot and Nine Inch Nails. Equilibrium returned. It was time to hit the streets.

I knew the folks next door to The Swamp at Rick's Sports Saloon, which was a strip club that had TVs for whatever game was on. Calling it a "sports bar" was a significant stretch. The only usage of the hips anyone was watching was on stage, not on the field. I was the ringer since I knew a bunch of people in the French Quarter. Some of these guys wanted a proper strip club experience, while others wanted the sketchy New Orleans you hear about in movies like *Easy Rider*. We agreed that the dudes who wanted the suit-and-tie, VIP booth situation could get theirs. They'd get to see the super pretty girls, spend an arm and a leg on overpriced drinks, and get hustled for lap dances—the same song and dance like every other club. The girls at Rick's were off the charts, which was to be expected in a place that costs $20 to walk inside. Thankfully, one of my homies was bartending, so the first round was on him and we didn't have to pay the cover charge.

Out of nowhere, I get a text from my cousin Bill, who was on a cross-country motorcycle trip with a friend. They'd landed in New Orleans and took me by surprise. They weren't planning on it, but the route worked out that way. I was psyched. I hadn't seen my cousin in a few years, and within thirty minutes, he was sitting with us in Rick's. His friend, who wasn't allowed to have fun because his wife sucked, was left sitting in the hotel room. Talk about divorce material.

We spent about an hour or so watching the natives twerk for dollars and solicit us for lap dances. Luckily, I was off the hook because they knew I worked next door. I can't stand getting hustled for lap dances. Fake stripper conversation is not my deal whatsoever. While everyone else was getting the hustle, I watched for free and checked the White Sox score. Hoss next to me was all falling in love with the Latina from Miami who *loved* his tattoos.

One of the guys leaned over to me and said, "Yo, so when are we going to see the real shit? You said you had a spot that was wild."

I did *indeed* have a spot that would give them a cheap thrill or two. Rick's was a snack before the fetid buffet I was about to lay on these fools. When everyone felt like they'd spent enough cash to put a few kids through Notre Dame, it was time to split. I spirited them down to where Chartres Street leads toward Canal. It's the stretch where Sneaky Pete's, Jimani, and Backspace sit, affectionately known as "Skid Row." What happens in these bars *stays* in these bars. If you're looking to wind up somewhere greasy in the middle of the night, look no further. You'll find what you're seeking. Back then, around the corner from Jimani was a small stretch on Iberville Street where there was a secret gay bathhouse called Rub & Tug. Next door, our destination: Dixie Divas.

Dixie Divas was a nightmare. It was the grimiest, low down nastiest joint in the French Quarter. It was the homeless, toothless, overweight, prison-tatted, distant cousin of Rick's. It was as bare-bones as a "strip club" could be. It was small, dirty, and always looked like a murder has just been Windexed off the chipped concrete floor. No one in their right mind went inside unless they were looking to cop or because they were into low-grade material.

The Chicago crew had gotten their wish. There's that moment when the record scratches in the movies? This was one of those. Me, my four friends with throat tattoos, and my ultra-normal-looking cousin were eager beavers, ready to play. The room stank like cigarettes from the

EXISTENTIAL THIRST TRAP

Bronze Age copulating with a distinct odor of regret and intermingled with the sadness of empty bottles of Jim Beam and no-name gin. One or two Miller Lite neons blinked in a broken daze, no doubt freebies from a bar long closed. No liquor rep would have given them new ones. The joint wasn't bigger than a glorified closet. The dancers didn't use a stage but danced on the bar. The ceiling was rigged with a strip of plexiglass so the ladies could put their hands on it and grind outward toward thirsty patrons. They didn't even have the standard golden pole. Instead, there was a long piece of industrial-grade pipe they could swing from. *Penthouse*, this most definitely was not.

Dixie Divas's clientele wasn't exactly what you'd call your high-dollar shoppers. Think bounty hunter crackheads. The place was frequented by the kind of gutter dwellers who looked like they'd been smoking methamphetamines on the hour for the last seventeen years; their buddy who "rode into town" was always alongside, sipping Wild Irish Rose out of a paper bag. With heads of unwashed hair and toothless smiles, these men kept the strippers alive with their patronage. It was a tragic place. The soundtrack to this C-section-scarred thirst trap was played off a small laptop plugged into a Radio Shack sound system.

Dixie Divas's tagline should have been something like "where strippers go to die" or "knife wounds allowed." The club was like the last little bits of grease left in the pan after frying some cheap bacon. The girls featured a broad selection of domestic dispute battle wounds and missing teeth. Some were so over the hill, they looked like Satan had given up running the meter long ago. Some looked like linebackers squeezed into rhinestone-studded tube tops and $16 heels.

Needless to say, my friends fell in love. The beers from Rick's were weighing on my bladder. I made my way back toward the bathrooms. As I opened the door, someone shouted, "Hey! I'm trying to do some fucking coke here!"

ROBERT DEAN

I shut the door and gave them their time to sniff. I was stuck waiting. While I lingered, the worst post-op stripper I've still seen to this day crawled out of the shadows and tapped me on the shoulder. I nearly jumped through the roof, but she was just letting me know I had to keep waiting because "a little boy and a little girl were busy in the bathroom." Christ. Look, I'm all for folks living their best lives and all that, but this woman was a fucking disaster. Her boob job was worth about $3.75 and a pack of Camels. It looked like a surgeon had rammed two tangerines under her skin and sewed it back twice as tight. She had fried-out black witch hair that was straight off the shelves of Spirit Halloween. To top it off, this lady had a face like a corrections officer. A pair of dead eyes were steeped in misery, while the sallow skin stretched across her skull was Botox-tight. Under her vacant eye sockets, violet circles protruded through caked-on makeup. She didn't bother to smile around the Kool that bent between her pink sparkly lips.

After the cokehead buzzed out of the bathroom, tipping his hat to me for letting him get his toot in peace, I finally got to piss. When I came out to find my friends, I walked past two men who looked like they'd crawled straight out from under a pile of needles in a heroin clinic talking to a stripper thicker than Honey Boo-Boo's mom at her worst. She didn't even attempt to go down by us. Instead, she sat with her legs swinging off the bar, talking to these guys drinking cans of the cheapest beer in the house. Their dirty beards and craggy smiles should have told her she wouldn't get rich off their patronage. I don't think she cared. The two skids eye-fucked her, and she clearly loved the low-rent attention.

The bartender working behind the bar looked like she was on her last neuron to burn. We were standing at the gates of hell, and she still had to try to sell beer. (One word on this bar. When I talk about it, some folks are like, "I've

EXISTENTIAL THIRST TRAP

been to the Clermont Lounge!" That's no big deal. Clermont is an Atlanta institution that's fun as hell. Dixie Divas was a thousand times worse. You have a great time in Clermont. Dixie Divas was a place to find cheap speed and get an STD.)

The stripper at the end of the bar pulled long tokes from her menthol and let the smoke bleed from her mouth as the bums gave her something better than cash: dignity in a place everyone looks down their nose at—Penthouse, this joint was not. A few other girls hung in the shadows. No one wanted to come by us. The stripper with the bad tits took one catwalk stroll past us, and once we started hooting and hollering, she walked right the fuck back. These dudes had money out, ready to throw it. The bartender was making her night's money; our posse was ordering rounds of shots and beers six at a time, continuously. But she still didn't want to mingle. She was overwhelmed.

I stepped onto Iberville Street for a minute to talk to my cousin, who needed a breather. We caught up on family drama for a minute and went back inside, knowing we were likely missing some chick with a peg leg or a half a face. When we got back inside, the boys were being entertained by a thick redbone with a fire engine red mohawk. She only danced to Rihanna songs and told us that was her stage name.

No, she did not look like Rihanna.

However, this Rihanna wannabe wanted it. She was game for *anything*. Her monthly bills were getting paid as fives, twenties, and tens flew at her. The four out-of-towners were front and center. She was pumping it at their faces and kept moving her panties aside to give them a look. Dollars began to get stuffed into orifices where money should not go. She writhed and moaned. She used every part of her body but her hands to collect her cash. I do believe she was having a good time with our circus. She was asking for the boys to do things to her in front of everyone.

ROBERT DEAN

The bartender, a tiny woman in her late 40s who likely hated her current life station and must have been doubling as a manager, was losing her fucking mind. These savages were slipping money *inside* of this woman.

"You can't do that! What are you doing! Oh my God!" she shouted.

As the real Rihanna's "S&M" played over the garbage speakers, *our* Rihanna was on her back, swimming in money. The take was easily a few hundred dollars.

"Shut the fuck up, bitch! You play whatever songs they want! I got kids to feed!"

She threw two twenties at the bartender, who looked defeated. She returned to letting one of the guys suck on her titties. The bartender put her head down and started popping open the beers, passed them to us as needed.

The house mom—the leader, I don't know—appeared next. She was gigantic and dressed in all black, looking straight-up like drag queen Darth Vader. She was damn close to my height and weight. Her hair was a black teased 80s tangle, while her lips were vodka-stained. I could see the mauve lipstick on her teeth. She looked like a tall-as-fuck goth Tiny Tim.

At first, she hovered. She watched and studied our actions. She wanted to know if she could sell us the goods on the secret menu. Some of the boys continued to wrap dollar bills around their fingers, and next thing, they'd disappear. With her back on the bar and her hips in the air, Rihanna invited them to play. It was one of the most disgusting things I've ever seen.

The house mom leaned over to the few of us *not* involved in the scrum and whispered with an air of crazed, sexual frenzy, "We could go upstairs and party. There are no cameras and no rules. We can cut you a deal on anything. No rules. It's fun upstairs, anything goes. We can get wild."

She stressed the *no rules* part. Yikes. We thanked her

EXISTENTIAL THIRST TRAP

for her offer and politely declined. My friends are many things, but they are not the type of dudes who bang garage-sale-priced strippers in a crack den.

Of course, you wouldn't know that to look at them. One of the guys in the posse had his face straight up in Rihanna's ass, right on the bar. Someone had the bright idea to pull out a camera and start snapping. Nothing says "Kodak Moment" like a large stripper's pock-scarred cheeks bouncing off your nose. The house mom had drifted away into the shadows again. The bartender tried to step in. Generally speaking, cameras are a No-No in strip clubs.

Rihanna shooed her away. "Bitch! Do you see this money?! Shut the fuck up."

The pictures and video got dirtier. Our girl played the part. After her songs finished, she slid off the "stage" and began to scoop up the cash she'd made in a few short minutes. She was flush for the month, easily. None of the other girls wanted anything to do with us. The "bar/stage" was vacant. We waited. Rihanna seemed annoyed. By now, we were shouting requests for songs by bands like Danzig, Deftones, and Sade. Anything to get the room extra horny.

"The fuck is y'all doing? We got paying customers down here!" Rihanna screamed, sticking her wad of cash in the cup of her bra.

Witch Hair took a deep breath, gave a smile, and made one more pass. The catcalls began, and she retreated back to the other end of the bar, refusing to come down by us.

Rihanna groaned. "These bitches complain about being broke. Fuck that. I'm getting mine."

As she gathered herself and made conversation, she casually wanted us to know that we could all "get our dicks sucked off for sixty each."

We passed. Twice, we'd been offered a private party.

Were we giving off a weird vibe? I don't know.

Eventually, the house mom came back with a new girl. Rihanna hung around, cornering one of the guys and letting him know she was into big boys. She made it crystal clear she'd give him a discount should he want her services. She even tried kissing him on the mouth.

Long minutes later, we still had no dancers. Rihanna was too busy flirting with the big boy, Witch Hair wasn't looking at us, and the other big girl had disappeared upstairs, into the land where morality went to die.

With no one else getting up on the pole, Andrew took it upon himself to become the entertainment. Whipping off his shirt and dropping his pants, he stumbled through "The Outsider" by A Perfect Circle, spinning around with about the same level of grace as the girls in this fetid hellhole. Getting down to only his underwear, he took to the bare pipe and put on the best show he could. The bartender had given up trying to contain the party. We were her only real customers, and no one with our money was about to walk in the door. She accepted it for what it was, while cash was thrown at her.

Finally, one of the girls crept out of the shadows and began to strut. She was cute, but you could tell she was on hard times. There was no other explanation for why she worked there. You could see the drugs swimming behind her eyes. Bad life choices. She was literally working a pipe in the worst bar in the city. That shit felt like an after school special, and it was hard to look at someone clearly on stuff that would knock out a Clydesdale as she ground her cha-cha on a random dude's nose for a few bucks.

I moved outside and started talking to my cousin. He was a part of the group but only a quiet observer. Drunk and only in town for the night, he jumped in with us for the kind of good time that his friends back home would never venture out for. A random dude was chatting us up when the guy who was in the bathroom earlier came by and slapped something into his hand. It was a folded-up dollar, like a little pocket.

"It's a dollar's worth of coke! Go do it, stupid!"

EXISTENTIAL THIRST TRAP

The guy vanished immediately. My cousin was downloading a lot of information at once: the club earlier, Rihanna, open drug use, the whole night. My friend Bryan came out to find us, taking a long sip from his old fashioned.

"You know when it's time to leave the party because shit gets weird?" he said.

"Yeah," I replied.

"We got asked to join an orgy. A hundred bucks a guy. I think it's time to go somewhere else."

When I looked back inside, the drugged-out stripper was making out with Rihanna. The music thumped as they felt one another up. It was probably best not to find out what happened upstairs.

My then-wife was pregnant with my kid. I had to get home and pretend I was a normal adult somehow, despite the obvious flaws in that logic. I wonder what all those girls are up to now that Dixie Divas is long gone, busted for drug and human trafficking and turning tricks. Those dollars aren't losing themselves in the ether, you know.

NO MATTER HOW HARD THEY TRY, A PLAYLIST WILL NEVER BE A MIXTAPE

I'M ENGAGED IN a battle in a comments donnybrook over the *Runaways* movie. Despite Lita Ford having a few hits, she'll forever be known as the chick who did "Close my Eyes Forever" with Ozzy Osbourne, growling in a smoky cave or some shit while Ozzy looks like a drag queen in the video. Aside from the obvious killers of "Bad Reputation" and "Do You Want to Touch Me" and being the blueprint for woman-fronted punk rock, Joan Jett produced the lone Germs record, and that alone makes her cool as fuck. There's also beefing over Iron Maiden, who sound like an army of balloon animals trotting over a hill while cartoon ducks fly pink and purple bomber planes while their whack mascot Eddie roams around dressed like a pirate to me. Black Sabbath prayed to goat heads laying in pentagrams made of salt. Judas Priest still rips as Rob Halford sports leather fuck-me suits while screaming about banging dudes. For my dollar, Heavy Metal is supposed to be scary, not cheerful. This is music nerd 101: argue about opinions and facts that no one else except the dorks in the dispute care about—the shit that women purr over, you know.

I read somewhere that part of what makes us human is our ability to laugh and to love music. I don't know if

EXISTENTIAL THIRST TRAP

that's bullshit or not, but I like that way it sounds. Banjo twangs and trap beats act as the heartbeat to my existence. I think about music constantly, so why wouldn't that assessment make sense? The obsession creeps into my everyday life in multiple forms, like when I buy bootleg Tribe Called Quest shirts off Instagram, or my best friend and I walk into the bar, he grabs the first round, and I load the jukebox with music that's objectively *good* vs. what a drunk dude from the suburbs wants to hear because some people live their lives putting Sublime's *40oz to Freedom* on repeat. If you don't do this, you will wind up hearing Crazytown's "Butterfly."

I ain't about that life.

Being a music nerd is a life sentence, it's an obsession of wanting to know how the Beastie Boys put together *Paul's Boutique*, getting into heated debates about how Aerosmith wrote better music while all geeked out on the shit, that James Brown is better than Elvis, how by *Low End Theory*, Phife could tangle with Q-Tip as a true competitor, and dropping the knowledge that no matter how much labor you might put into it, a playlist will never be a mixtape.

Some of my favorite memories are going with my friends to a record store, browsing the stacks, checking out what was hocked in the used bin hoping to find that holy grail copy of Tom Waits' *Rain Dogs* or an O.G. copy of the Misfits's *Walk Among Us*. Nag Champa floated in the air, purging the smell of day shift weed smoked. We had four different record stores in my area on the south side of Chicago. Each store had a different vibe, a different flow, you had to know how the stores worked, how to be cool under the judgy eyes of the clerks. The experience is what matters in music appreciation, we celebrate the journey. Record stores still exist, but so does Amazon. You can find whatever you want with a click. Knowing that Space Lord Bezos will have your copy of Parliament Funkadelic's

Maggot Brain delivered to your door is convenient, but it does take the fun out of the search.

I'm caught in that generation of folks who can adapt to technology but remember when call waiting was the new thing. With evolutions happening by the minute, there's a pang of regret, lost in the forgetfulness of touchstones that we once loved but have faded into memories. Sadly, many times they're the things we don't immediately think of when someone brings up "remember back in 1996 when the Fugees *The Score* record dropped?"

I'm 40 now. I remember Pearl Jam and Digable Planets being new sounds. I remember when we cared about the radio. My kids care about YouTube.

A mixtape was an act of love, a symbol that they gave the utmost fuck about you. You gotta understand, we didn't have Facebook groups. There were no hashtags. You either liked someone's shirt at a concert, in a smokey late-night diner, or met in the halls of your school. The communal bonding experience of discovering the other freak who liked early Ministry or the deep cuts of KRS-One wasn't exactly like knowing who raced home to watch TRL. The mixtape generation was from the mid-1980s, when black cassettes became affordable, all the way until we saw the rise of the iPod in the mid-to-late 2000s.

A playlist has its place. A playlist has a purpose. When Spotify shows me playlists, many times, they're outstanding, and when I'm driving, poking my finger at the screen, they're just what I need—accessibility. There are benefits to utilizing the technology of ease that a playlist offers. If you want to hear an algorithm-driven mix of the best punk from the Midwest, it exists, the same goes if you're dying to dive into Dolly Parton's B-sides.

A playlist is not a love letter, a dare, or a wish in audio format. It's copy and pasting. Mixtapes aren't a collection of songs. They're an introduction to who you are. Makeups, breakups, and make outs happened from these pieces of

EXISTENTIAL THIRST TRAP

alchemy. Friendships were formed and alliances were cemented. When you made a mixtape, you had to own all of the music you wanted to feature, or you at least had to have a dual tape deck to dub a side of the cassette that someone might have made for you. Unlike a playlist where one can be compiled, the songs juked around, a mixtape was an order, a flow, a collection of music you NEEDED someone to hear, if as an act of friendship, "check out these bands, I think you'll love them," but as an extension of the self.

The magic about a mixtape was that if the recipient was into Nirvana but only knew the big radio bands, this is where your deep music nerd knowledge cemented everything. My move was giving something a little familiar so what you'd share could be a bridge into the possible. The sonic roux was there, so my spice was dropping tracks like "Waiting Room" by Fugazi, "Here Comes Your Man" by The Pixies, a little Naked Raygun, Melvins, the Misfits, Sonic Youth, The Jesus Lizard (admittedly a deep cut pick, but there had to be chaotic balance).

But then, there were complicated layers from there on out. What if that Nirvana tape was for a girl, and she liked how thoughtful you were, and then you started making out with her on the regular? The rules changed. The mixtape acted as a continual barometer of season, emotional state, and mood. What if you discovered that she loved dancier stuff? Then you had to take stock of what you had that you could swing to—maybe Michael Jackson, Boney M, Prince, or Justin Timberlake? Maybe she loved techno, or disco; you had to find out how to make it work, you had to dig. What if you were bummed out and wanted to share how you felt without saying it, a tokenized "this is my mood" in hopes someone would get the drift when you were categorizing a successive string of bummer songs in a row, Robert Smith and the Cure be damned?

There was the tracklist and potential artwork, which

had to say "no, I'm not a fucking psycho" without serial killer scrawl and potentially weird drawings. Some folks went to levels of crafting full-blown folk art pieces by cutting up magazines for their tracklists.

And when you finally handed the goods over, you had to wait. You were dying to know if they liked the tape. Did they love it all? Maybe a few songs. Some people put it right on in the car, while others let the collection fester, depending on the relationship. I did want to know if you liked Joe Jackson's "Steppin' Out" on my 80s dance party mix. What if the recipient took the tapes knowing that they didn't give a fuck about them, they were humoring you? Talk about hell. I've heard such threats issued during a breakup: "I never even listened to those stupid CDs you made me!" And for a dork who can catalog Pearl Jam's drummers or the nine members of Wu-Tang, that hurts like being told you've got a small dick.

The idea of a mixtape endures is that it's a thunderbolt in the night, banged loudly by Joe Strummer screaming, "what are we gonna do now?" That moment shared was a whisper no one else could hear, even if we cranked the volume on a broken stereo. In an era with so many things built for ease of use, comfort, and disposal, taking the time seems quaint but also emotionally necessary when the little things really do matter.

BATHROOM CODE

SOME PLACES ARE shared spaces. The vibes I'm talking about are when you hit a punk bar in Malaysia and you're screaming along to the Misfits with a chick who doesn't speak the same language but knows all the words to "Hybrid Moments." That shit is straight magical. Next thing you know, you're wandering the back streets with locals, looking for trouble.

Those moments of shared majesty are amazing. You're loaded in a small town in the middle of nowhere, Texas, and no one is talking shop or politics. You're sitting on a curb eating gooey grilled cheese and a king-sized greasy bag of fries, happy as hell. People are chatting, swaying in line, and you're feeling good. Each suck of the straw releases your chocolate milkshake down the hatch, and the joint is playing Bruce Springsteen. That's a moment everyone can get into. If not, they're assholes.

However, there are exceptions. Mainly in public bathrooms. One of the most agreed-upon vibe observation practices is the bathroom, specifically the men's room. Women's restrooms are like social clubs. They share lip gloss. If someone needs a tampon, they can call an audible. Girls compliment one another. They keep a community-driven atmosphere. I hear it's a nice place to hang out.

The men's room is not like this whatsoever. It's a shared *Fortress of Solitude* and as silent as a library, give or take a few grunts and farts. No matter where you are—

in a small town or Los Angeles or Chaing Mai—fellas do not want to chat while holding their dicks. This isn't even just a straight guy thing. I've been in plenty of gay bars where they also observe this code of silence, even if it's a little less stringent. Minutes ago, boys are out on the dance floor in sparkly purple hot pants, calling one another Queen Bitches and shit. The minute we're in the commode, all that pageantry *stops*.

In the men's room, we do not chat. We do not mingle. We only take the urinal next to one another if it's unavoidable. We stare in silence at the tile square in front of us, and we do not move our eyes unless it's downward, toward the piss stream. Now, we do love peeing *on* things in the urinal. If there's a slip of paper in there, we'll try our best to kill the fibers and turn that paper into mush. You could put a photo of a dude's mom in there; I promise he's not going to try and save her. On the contrary, he's going to try to burn her face off with used beer. If it's a one-man unit and someone leaves comet streaks of shit in the bowl, every man who comes in after will shoot their piss straight at those turd chunks, trying to laser that doo-doo from the porcelain.

The same goes for a trough. We *love* pissing in those, especially ones filled with ice. Wanna see guys light up like a Christmas tree? Take them to a bar and don't tell them there's a trough in there filled with ice. The first guy to take a leak will come out and tell the table, as excited as a prepubescent boy who just saw a pair of tits for the first time since infancy.

There's a shared experience of just "knowing" what's up, and then you and a stranger low fist bump out of respect. It's the Misfits. It's the ice in the trough. I love that shit. In this world, we ain't got much, but damn, does taking a long drunk piss feel good. Some would almost say it can be better than busting a nut. All I know is you'd better watch out if you drop a photo of your mom in the

EXISTENTIAL THIRST TRAP

toilet, we're coming for her, or your brother, or that book of matches. There are no safe targets where the pee is coming in hot, literally.

FEED MY SOUL

FEW THINGS STIR the mojo, rile up the gut, and are as goddamned religious as the intoxicating fumes of carne asada summoning life on a hot grill. The street taco is something that brings people to their knees. No matter what you love or what you believe in, this street food changes everything. The scent drives screws into your soul. It reminds us that there's a reptilian brain buried down past our simian love of drive-thru iced lattes and comfortable pairs of Adidas.

Flesh over fire is a social gospel, exacted in real-time. Passers-by, they can't help it. One whiff, they're digging in their pockets for a few bucks to maybe grab one or two off the taco man for the road. This is a sacred and holy position: us plebeians down here, we thank you, taco man.

Food is powerful like that. It does things to our social chemistry. It empowers our soul. Food is the cross-generational salve that takes the pain out of a sting. When it's a birthday, we celebrate with cake. When someone kicks the bucket, we mourn them with fried chicken or food made by old ladies at a church. It doesn't matter what country you're in or what caste you belong to, there is no higher place of love and respect, of conversation, than the meal. From foxholes to chefs ready to battle a Saturday night during regular times, good food exists without pretext because it's honest.

For me, 2020 was like getting kicked in the heart with

EXISTENTIAL THIRST TRAP

baseball cleats. Repeatedly. We're all dealing. Social injustice. Coronavirus. Mental health issues roaring like a starved tiger, dragging a lot of us to the edge of sanity. It's been a vicious year.

I struggled for weeks with putting my thoughts together. What can anyone say in the face of the kind of devastation 2020 was serving? What purpose does anyone's voice serve during a time full of revolutionary moments that was also a recurrent nightmare for the restaurant and bar industry—all while locked into a personal roller coaster of emotions? My best take was that the year was a complicated time—one we'll make it past, but not without some scars. Which is why I drifted back to food. I stayed burned out for weeks, staring at my laptop screen, wondering how I was going to write. Everything felt like a broken ball bearing case inside a skateboard wheel. Instead of forward motion, I stalled, metal grinding on metal.

For a hot minute, I didn't know if I had any gas left in the tank. It was fucking *bleak*. Food was the connective tissue that felt honest. Cooking made me feel like there was something more. It was earnest. Not forced. Food gave me a starting point. It was my way of talking honestly.

The kitchen is a place to make a small change in our world. Food is the great equalizer: it can humble us but always teaches us. A kitchen is a universal place constructed via honesty, hard work, and transparency, the things everyone believes in. If you want to learn something about yourself, walk up to the stove and try to keep pace with a grandmother who can break a chicken down quicker than you can FaceTime a pal from work. Ask the guy who knows what's the secret to good crawfish and you won't get a one-word answer, you'll get a college-level course in flavor profiling. This is a mantra.

But, here's the thing: food is ultimately political. The best things we eat, the foods we love, most of them came from struggle. The dishes we revere today came from the leftover crap no one wanted. Brisket, beans and rice, box macaroni and cheese, oysters, sushi, foie gras, caviar, skirt steak, escargot, carnitas, and po' boys are all working-class creations. They were served with whatever was on hand to get through the day. Someone who was starved like a dog had to use their noodle to figure out how the hell to make crawfish a staple. Lobsters? Sea-bugs. They were fed to prisoners, while soul food comes from the scraps of slavery. Anyone who pretends otherwise is lying to themselves, and you, about what's good and why.

We can learn a lot about people through their cuisines. That's why food drives us forward. Food creates harmony. It cuts the bullshit. These "outsider" foods became high dollar menu items because the story changed around them, but the outcome was the same: they brought strange bedfellows.

I have a belief that good food changes how we see one another, that two bitter enemies can find joy if they're open to it. Could we take a conservative and a progressive and sit them down for a meal without making it about politics but about two people's reactions? I think we could. For one hour, it could be just about the food. A good meal strips away the context for a moment, giving people a chance to celebrate something together.

More folks need to meet over a plate of Nashville hot chicken, talk, sweat it out, and laugh at how their mouths are on fire. This is real sweat equity. For those few minutes, it's two people eating together, grunting and groaning in appreciation. Breaking bread together breaks a cycle of prejudice based on cultural differences. Instead of folks immediately hating on each other, a good meal creates a shared language. Maybe after these two have wiped their brows, talked, and heard each other's stories, they can find a place to see where they disagree, why they feel the way they do about life, but ultimately work together to change

EXISTENTIAL THIRST TRAP

it. It's through those stories that we can see our humanity through life's clearest lens.

Injustice requires action. It takes people out in the streets, along with the government getting its act together too. But if there's one small way the culinary community can champion togetherness, this is the weapon of choice. This is radical action, one plate at a time.

WHAT'S YOUR HUSTLE?

DO WHAT YOU LOVE, they said. Well, my first job wasn't precisely strip-searching Victoria's Secret models. No, I wasn't running numbers for the mafia or selling forgeries on the black market. Instead, I was a Penny Saver delivery boy. Every week, I stuffed a pile of papers into thin orange sleeves and tossed them on just about every porch in a two-mile radius. I'd sling the massive sack with the uncomfortable strap across my shoulder and hit the streets, usually on my skateboard. Block by block. You could hear me coming as my wheels hit each break in the concrete slabs—*thump, thump, thump.*

I didn't mind throwing the papers. That part was fun. What sucked was the collecting of money. I hated that. People were always assholes when you tried to collect the monthly five dollars they owed to know who had garage sales or if someone's cocker spaniel, Yoda, was missing.

My first real introduction to sex came on that paper route. I lived in Oak Forest, a semi-suburban town outside of the Chicago city limits. It was twilight, folks were making dinner, and cars were heading home from work. I got over to Ridgeland Avenue, the main thoroughfare, with constant vehicles coming and going. I was not expecting to see a couple going at one another like a hammer and nails in plain view. There, in a bedroom window, with the curtains wide open, facing the street clear as day, a guy

EXISTENTIAL THIRST TRAP

fucked the ever-loving shit out of his lady friend. And not an *oopsie* while two people screwed missionary. No, like my ten-year-old ass stood there with my jaw on the sidewalk while this man defiled this woman doggystyle, tits against the window, putting on a straight-up Doing The Nasty tutorial for me. She rode him, he threw her ankles around his neck, and I watched every minute of it like a real pervert.

How no one else saw this was a miracle. No one was out walking their dogs. Also, this was in the 1990s, so people weren't out "getting their cardio." For what seemed like an eternity, these two fucked like dogs and let me stare in amazement. After they climaxed, they killed the lights and shut the curtains. Every day, as long as I lived in that neighborhood, I always looked in that window. I never saw a freak mode session ever again.

I didn't last long on the paper route. There's something that grosses me out about how some people's houses smell.

I guess you could say I've always had a contentious relationship with work. Writing is all I've wanted to do since I was seventeen. I don't have any real skills, aside from writing, throwing papers, and collecting the odd traumatic experience. At this point, I'm like a pirate, jumping from job to job because when you're a writer, you get fired, laid off, or let go. I've gotten used to it. I don't know if I'm more of a "professional working writer" or "professional fuck-up." I've been on unemployment more times than I'd like to admit. About once a week, I'll catch my reflection in the mirror, wondering what the hell I am doing. Was this road worth it?

I started as a paperboy, but as an adult, I don't know how to do much other than work in a bar. That basically amounts to yelling at people in a microphone to get drunk or playing songs to get drunk on Bourbon Street. I got shit-hammered every day and somehow managed to stay employed for almost six years. How, I have no idea.

ROBERT DEAN

We were savages on Bourbon. This was before everyone had a dream of being on YouTube, and no one was on Instagram yet. What happened, you know, was a little bit of everything. I experienced the consequences of living in the moment. Sorority girls flashed us. Copious amounts of drugs were bought, sold, and done in the DJ booths. Everyone who was an entertainer fooled around in every booth on the street, on the job, and right in front of customers.

As a lifestyle, being an entertainer was perfect for me. I can make my way through rapping a Wakka Flakka bar on "Hard in the Paint" during Essence Fest, but do I know how to deal with HR requirements? Ha. I used to start my day hungover with a coffee that could strip every good piece of bacteria from my stomach and then down two triple shots of Jameson just to get warmed up for my shift. Moving to Austin and learning how to operate like an average person, a person who isn't going to catch strangers fucking in the workplace bathroom and buy them celebration shots with the bar applauding them on the way out—let's say, it was challenging. I don't think I was built to work in the white-collar world. I'm too adapted to the low life. Part of me still belongs down on Bourbon.

It's not that I haven't tried. Apparently, my resume is good enough for me to get an interview, but when I open my mouth, the recruiter realizes I just want to work and be left alone. Then, there's a problem. I ask for feedback, never get it. I ask questions and get the safety answers. The corporate world is spineless. I don't speak their language, and they don't speak mine. I keep showing up, resume in hand, because honestly? They pay and I need the money.

The jobs I've had up to this point have been all over the place, but none have lent me any real-life skills. In high school, I kept the same job working at a movie theater, and let me tell you, that was some wild shit.

My friends worked at this movie theater. First, it was a

EXISTENTIAL THIRST TRAP

Cineplex Odeon, and then it became Loews Cinema. To say we ran that business into the ground would be putting it lightly. This was the late 90s; we didn't have fast computers. We had ancient machines with green displays for basic math and ticket sales. We signed our names in pen. We clocked in with a rudimentary system that could be cheated, and there were zero security cameras. Everything was the honor system. You can guess how that went.

When I first got there, we had projection operators, but they canned them and made *us* do it—a bunch of kids, aged 17 to 19. Sure, we all got how to spool the movie eventually, and some of us learned how to put the movies together—because back in olden times, movies came on film, on these gigantic reels that we had to tape together manually. After we taped the reels, we had to watch the film to make sure it worked. This became a ritual: to hang out and to bring all of our friends in late-night to watch it too. When *the Blair Witch Project* came out, we showed it on two screens and invited everyone we knew, thus robbing the theater of thousands of dollars in unsold tickets. Someone was cleaning the upstairs and found a hidden copy of Pink Floyd's *The Wall*, so naturally, it was pieced together too. We charged $5 for a midnight showing, and you could bring in whatever substance you wanted.

We set up the red velvet ropes and threw wrestling matches in the lobby. We stole money left and right with a scheme for selling half of a ticket stub and keeping the cash. Some of the people who worked there stole so much money they could have paid for college. Me, I only took enough to buy CDs and concert tickets. I'm also terrible at math, and the whole thing freaked me out. We were dirtbags, through and through.

One of the other employees always greeted customers with the phrase "how may I service you," which no one caught on to. I let pretty girls in for free. I let guys with cool band shirts in for free. We traded movie passes—the kind you're supposed to hand out when the film breaks down—to every restaurant in the area for free food. Our boss used to fuck her boyfriend in the office. It was like being in Kevin Smith's *Clerks*. One of the girls who worked there started hanging out with a top-hatted guy who unironically wore a bandana tied around his knee. He decided to throw a séance in the middle of the lobby during a shift. I wasn't working, but I had come to see *Fear and Loathing in Las Vegas* with my friends.

Walking past his voodoo scene, I asked, "What the fuck are you weirdos doing?"

The séance didn't turn up any ghosts. It wasn't haunted, just a movie theater with four screens, one of which was playing the Pokemon movie.

I worked at the Chicago Board of Trade for a few years too. I tried to get up into the marketing team as a writer, but that gig never happened. So, I ended up working the pits, back when they were a madhouse complete with people screaming in one another's faces, choking each other with their ties. I saw greed every day. I watched millionaires bet on who would fuck the new runners that came every summer from college. People got the hotfoot with a match, just like the cartoons. A longstanding story was about one broker's clerk who got banged in the bathroom one day using a ketchup packet for lube. I saw fights, guys employed as a front for low key drug deals, binge drinking after work, insider trading, money moving from broker calls into trading accounts for someone's kid.

Once, this dude who was a summer hire, a total fuck-up burnout, went to the ATM for some cash; he left his receipt, and I found it. There was thirty grand in his checking account because his daddy was a trader. At the time, I was living off of ramen and the occasional free drink that came my way whenever a broker would be cool and buy the rounds. That job was the perfect teeing off for life

EXISTENTIAL THIRST TRAP

in New Orleans. I wasn't sleeping already, but God, I was the worst card counter on earth. I could collect cards and check trades with the best of them, even negotiate the prices for my guys, but when it came to back-office work, making sure the numbers worked, I was terrible. I could barely do the math, let alone find needles in haystacks like that. So, in the end, it was my first time getting fired and the kick in the ass to be like, *finally, you're a writer. Worry about Flannery O'Conner, not whatever the fuck is going on in the market.*

And now, I exist on paper. What kind of adult has a work history like this? I can write and be a fuck up. Congrats to me.

I lose jobs, get jobs, and chase the creative dragon. Every writer shares that belief, the hope that someday they won't have any corporate masters. I dream of *my* schedule, just being me. I don't know what it is, but whoever's hiring to fill a cubicle can smell it on me. I don't care about getting together for a happy hour. I don't care about "office culture." I don't care about anything other than doing my work and going home.

I got laid off again in the middle of the pandemic, like so many other people. Did it suck? Yes it did, even if I didn't love it. Holding onto work during the Worst Year Ever was rough, considering Rome was burning all around me. My job was the boat of sanity I could sit in while the waves of bullshit crashed all around. Pre-pandemic, I had just separated from my wife, so my emotional health wasn't in tip-top shape. But then millions of people were getting sick, the economy took a nosedive, and well, the world changed. When everything around you sucks and people are on the news crying about potential homelessness and unemployment checks that don't come, you're thankful as hell that you're not with them—until you are.

As jobs go, the one that laid me off wasn't too bad. I

was writing for a startup, which is the type of gig that comes with a litany of headaches thanks to fluctuating budgets and constant directional pivots. Still, it was steady work. When the first COVID-19 wave hit, the company took the attitude of "we're going to get through this," but as we switched gears again and again, I started to get an unsettling feeling. I've seen this story before. Anyone who lives in Austin and works in the creative field has likely worked with startups. And there are always trappings on when something lingers in the air—hierarchy shuffles, people aren't as optimistic, and senior folks start quietly bailing out. Those are the obvious moves that made my spidey sense tingle, but with COVID, everything was remote. I couldn't pick up on the office vibes, the shortened conversations that would ordinarily make me think, *I know what's happening here.* Instead, I was just checking Slack or email and surviving like everyone else.

Frankly, I was happy to be working, to see the direct deposit hit every two weeks and sigh, knowing I was still in the fight, that I might see the crisis through in one piece.

It was not to be. The startup saw their entire business change overnight. Leadership rose to meet the challenges of an old model rooted in hospitality, restaurants, and events, which died with a viral disease shotgun blast. Because the infrastructure was there, we managed to help out workers and grocery stores to keep people fed across the nation. It was legitimately a point of pride. Like all things, though, the market settled. We bought time.

Then, in July of 2020, I had a full-blown depressive episode. The weight of my divorce, the lack of human interaction, my work having less value, and my stalled career felt like a Terminator robot foot on my skull. I couldn't get out of bed. What little I wrote was the smatterings of a broken man. To be fair to my ex-bosses, my breakdown was *not* my best work. I could barely look at a computer, let alone forge thoughts on an entirely new

EXISTENTIAL THIRST TRAP

industry with any authority, or even muster a fake-it-till-you-make-it scenario.

When the CEO put time on my calendar, I knew it was a wrap. Startup CEOs don't make house calls; they swing the ax. When you're the lone creative in an organization trying to survive a nearly company-killing event, you're the head on the block. Creatives are expensive and we're expendable. Site copy, content, media placements—all that can kick rocks when developers need to keep the business moving, even if it's at a glacial pace. When I was given my walking papers, it was an exhale. On one hand, I'd been professionally empty; but at the same time, I needed consistent money. My personal life was a minefield, and I've got kids.

I got severance. Unemployment took forever to hit. The State of Texas-authorized amount made me cringe. Punishing Americans for losing their jobs during a crisis is appalling. Millions were without safety nets, and that seemed to be totally fine with elected leaders. There were deferments available, but I had to put them on my credit cards, which I jacked up thanks to spending $11,000 on an amicable divorce, along with a new MacBook Pro that was the price of a used Nissan. I got a deferment on my car note too.

Over the next few months, I applied to over 100 jobs, both remote and local. I applied for jobs I was overqualified for in hopes they'll hire me as a freelancer. There were lots of rejection letters. Sometimes, I got to round two interviews. References or the round three interviews? Nope. And no offers. I got told I'm too experienced or too expensive. Sometimes recruiters didn't even show up. And then there were the Zoom meetings. Good Lord. If I never have another video conference, I will die a happy man.

Being a broke senior creative person kills me. It's not like I'm new at this, or untested. Yet, there's no clear career ladder, no hierarchy, and no guarantees. Like, I interviewed President Obama and have written for Apple but ask myself: Can you afford that falafel wrap for lunch? You've got soup at home, you know.

I'm not unique. This is the American Experience. We're stuck in this self-perpetuating hell. We keep looking for jobs. We want to work. There are only so many gigs to fill, and that number seems to change in response to the constant rollercoaster news on coronavirus recovery. We're all just holding our dicks and waiting for the brass in the White House to do the right thing, release unemployment funding, and take care of the people they allegedly represent. Until then, I'm still applying and expecting the absolute worst.

At least I have options outside my field. I'm about to be a line cook to make extra cash till an intrepid manager hires me. Who doesn't want a writer working the grill who reads French existentialist essays for enjoyment? I'd rather sit on park benches and daydream, but that ain't reality. I've got bills to pay in a broken America. Who wants a burger? Deep thoughts come free, but an extra slice of cheese is extra.

A COFFEE SHOP IN STRANGE CITY

THE PANDEMIC MADE me miss people. I miss dumb jokes live in person, groaning at my friends. I miss the way women laugh, the small talk we've all but cut off for fear of infection. Tell me all your shit. I need someone to relate to, otherwise, I'm gonna scream.

2020 was like a jacked-up *Twilight Zone* episode, but not a good one—a shitty remake with no plot. It seemed like we were all walking through life with two shoes on: *stay the fuck away from me* and *come over and make out, I trust you.*

Remember concerts? Remember fun? I do.

This experience has made me long to get that tangible, social, public piece of my humanity back. 2020 gave me a lot of time to think about simple pleasures, what makes me smile. I've taken multiple weird-ass journeys down the rabbit hole. Like, the weird late-night rabbit hole you don't tell people about. I've moved down there. I live in Strange City now.

I think about food, the past, and one particular cultural cornerstone: diner food. I miss diner culture. I miss that push and pull of drunk strangers, locals, and staff that move like an orchestra but with really good chili. When I lived in Chicago and New Orleans, we had all-night, 24/7 greasy spoons to grab a plate of shit slathered over eggs. I knew where to get that double cheeseburger cooked under a hubcap at three a.m.

The smell of fried eggs, coffee, old books, and cigarette smoke is the American Experience. The tinkle of a spoon hitting the sides of a porcelain diner mug is trapped in the psyches of everyone we know. We sign our names with grease in this country, one crinkle-cut French fry at a time. There isn't much your local diner hasn't seen. From bullet holes to broken hearts and the blue plate special, these places were a haven for another lost generation of kids looking for fuck-ups like themselves.

Now, a diner is a diner; a coffeehouse is a *coffeehouse*. People go to those joints to *work*. The person click-clacking away at their keys in a coffeehouse has *goals*. They're doing something, or trying to. People produce things. They hold conversations and respond to emails while sipping seven-dollar mocha-choca-bullshit in a cup that's three quarters ice. The baristas flex steaming and steeping skills to a symphony of hisses and pops. A diner, on the other hand, is where ridiculous ideas burst into life, where cups of coffee are sipped in contemplation. The life of a diner weirdo doesn't start till after the squares have hit the hay. Diner people take over booths after the crow flies and argue about John Waters flicks till the servers switch shifts. When you're sitting longways in a diner booth, the heels of your shoes kissing the seat's vinyl, that's where plans hatch. With each passing cup of coffee, the tension and excitement move like a dance because this is no longer a conversation. It's a war room for hopes and dreams. Some folks devise making their low budget masterpiece, while others scribble notes for their Great American Novel.

For the record, both these places are distinct from your local watering hole. When you sit in a bar, conversations lose their spark. The people who were so sharp or so dreamy under the influence of caffeine become sloppy with each swallow of cheap tequila or vodka flavored like Skittles. Good ideas become bad jokes, and losing the plot happens more often than not. I drank alone enough during

EXISTENTIAL THIRST TRAP

the quarantine. I was blacked out texting or hitting Facetime when I should have been long in the sack. Most of the folks I messaged were normal, trying to lead some kind of special "quarantine edition" life. They weren't thrilled to hear from me after hours, a fucking werewolf in Adidas shorts watching stand up specials, feeling super lonely while chugging Jameson.

Worst of all, there was no hangover breakfast the next day. Without diner coffee, are you even really drinking? Why does the coffee taste better in a diner than anywhere else in the world? Some say it's because the servers have their concoction just right, but they'd probably admit it's because they never wash the pots, which end up tasting like dirt and dinosaur bones. Diner coffee has notes of chipped cups, mangy silverware, and the old-timer who hangs at the register for an eternity, watching over his waffle and pork chop kingdom one dollar at a time.

The diner is a sanctuary; they never close; they never ask for anything in return, except a tip. They might take a few hours off so the kids can open their presents on Christmas, but come dinnertime, someone's slapping a ribeye on the griddle. It's always showtime at the joint where the servers show up tired of your bullshit, tired of everyone's bullshit. I can see them now: pens stuck in hair, feet aching, hustling past the handful of customers reading the newspaper or studying the menu like a Barthes essay. The lights in the diner never dim because they're open 24/7, just as the sign promises. If heaven has many islands, the one I love most will serve late-night pancakes.

NEW ORLEANS HARD

I HAVE A weird kind of love-hate relationship with New Orleans. It's like *The Notebook* meets *Sid & Nancy*. When I was leaving that city, I watched the clock, itchy to get on the road. I was prepared to get on with my life. I was ready to dip my toes into the waters of life that didn't come in a To-Go cup. Now that I'm gone? I miss that cesspool. But, fuck, living in New Orleans isn't easy.

I miss the crack heads, the brass bands, the hustlers, broken sidewalks, busted politicians, the con men, and the ice cream man who wants a tip while his tune has a bass beat. I miss the scary-ass dudes who lived down the block, the hood cats roaming the streets, and a whole city of people who don't know any better.

When I watch the news and see the bars on Bourbon Street getting busted over shot girls and door guys selling drugs, it doesn't shock me. It brings back fond memories. When they interview folks feigning surprise, that's complete bullshit. Door guys and shot girls have run drug rings for years. Everyone's got a piece in the game on Bourbon. The hustle is a part of New Orleans's DNA—if you got caught, it means you screwed up. Pirates founded that city. Do you think its tune is going to change? Hell no. People in New Orleans come up from nothing, pretty much everywhere, all the time. You heard of "Boston Strong." That ain't shit compared to "New Orleans Hard."

A few years back, I was visiting, standing in front of the

EXISTENTIAL THIRST TRAP

Dive Bar on Toulouse chatting with friends somewhere around two in the morning when we heard the familiar *pop-pop-pop* of gunfire. Instinctively, I grabbed my friend Patrick and threw him into the bar, slamming the wooden shutters behind us as we laid on the floor. Some of my other friends made it into the other door, while others kissed the concrete between cars. Nine shots rang out. Seven people were injured. Why? A guy got mad over someone smudging his sneakers. The dude pulled out his pistol, shitfaced, and fired into the crowd. Once we heard the sirens, we opened the doors back up. Not a minute before.

Once, on Halloween night, I worked at the Swamp when someone was killed literally on our doorstep. We'd just let a private party out when we heard the chaos. When the doors were opened, a body lay on the same threshold that I walked over every day to walk into the building. Police marked off the body and bullets while we milled around for a few hours inside the bar, watching the homicide squad doing their thing from the balcony. Living in New Orleans, you forge a bond with death. It's part of New Orleans. When you experience your first shooting, it's scary. When you're on your fifth or sixth, you know how to deal. I can't say I miss the sound of sirens and gunshots every day, but I do miss the vibrant sense of chaos lingering in the air like bad drugs. I get back often enough, but when I leave, I look like Mia Wallace riding home silently in Vincent Vega's keyed convertible, makeup smeared, a little blood on my lip, and a head full of demons. Exactly how the trip should be.

FREE STATE

I SHARED A bottle of cheap wine with a painter. I was down in my hideaway, Galveston Island. We sat in his studio garage swapping war stories, one glass at a time. He told me about pedaling a bike around paradise, making a living by splashing a rainbow of paint against the world.

He told me about island drunks who knew to come by on "Art Walk" nights because they knew they could mingle with the tourists in plain sight while catching a buzz, thanks to free bottles everywhere meant to lure rich people into comfort.

We talked about the Beatles, sex, and how one man's dream is another's nightmare.

We took dark dives into the ether, knowing the folks around us were just pretending when they said the world wasn't crumbling beneath their feet. It's a free state. A free fall. The painter and I understood that was the reason the whiskey hit harder. The fear made our bottles seem a little less empty.

I laid on his stained pull-out couch, reading about politics, about the probable end of the world. All points of view pointed to the apocalypse. Benches became confessionals, a place to share conversations with strangers. A pirate told me about "island jobs." Everyone was getting out or getting stuck. Dwelling on hard questions, we let the universe come with its claws out.

This was my kind of communion. I left relieved, the

EXISTENTIAL THIRST TRAP

brief break in my sanity slowly closing up again. It was night, so I walked down to the water, alone. The ocean tickled my feet, and I went for miles along the line where the wave breaks and falls gently to the shore.

For a minute there, I was free.

PART TWO:
ROTTEN HEART

BARE SOUL

TRYING TO DUST off from the hot fart that was 2020, I made a critical decision to switch from the regret machine known as Jameson over to Jager's friendlier, less pukey grown-up cousin, Fernet. Thanks to this life-changing, anxiety, self-worth, and depression-fighting upgrade, I had a shot at remaining emotionally coherent in 2021. Off Jameson, I wouldn't send desperate pleas for attention via texts and DMs when I could barely string together a cohesive train of thought, let alone try to come off as anything in the zip code of remotely cool. Another bonus point of semi-responsible drinking is that I haven't been out of my mind trying to stay up till 10 a.m., watching sad Christmas movies alone. Ordinary people would see this as a cry for help. I see it as a professional upgrade. I'm drinking soda, water, and bitters instead of killing bottles of beer between shots too. This was life at almost forty. People my age need to think about hydration.

Because I'm a certified adult who was keeping it together, I waited until I had the night off from my kids before I went on a bender. I hit all of my friends' happy hour shifts. I had parking lot tacos. I woke up in a good mood, with no missed phone calls or texts. My head wasn't pounding. When I got up to pee from drinking so much water, I turned my ringer on: I knew I had to get my boys at some point but didn't know exactly when.

Once the call came in and established the time, I

fucked off again. My digital leash immediately went into Silence is Golden mode. I didn't roll my fat ass out of bed till after 2 p.m. When I finally got up, I slouched around the house like a stack of possums in a trench coat. I did brush my teeth and shower, though. (Even at my most slovenly, I still wash my ass and crotch daily, if not twice. *Ladies*.)

I did do one productive thing and go for a run. I was trying to get post-divorce fuckable—Tinder is hard enough when you've got kids, a divorce, and are a weirdo looking for nirvana. Running helped me get used to this rollercoaster. It helped me ignore the fact that I was basically trying to "fuck around and find out," but like, on a spiritual level. If I was a real grownup, I'd have a tidy bank account, a career path, probably a house. Instead, 2021 made it even more obvious that I have no idea what I'm doing. Here's the director's cut of my transferable life skills:
- Can write
- Knows stuff about music
- Expert knowledge about the Chicago White Sox
- Can cook
- Enjoys doing the dishes and folding laundry
- Seeking nirvana

That's pretty much what it came to. I bullshitted my way through everything else. Frankly, I was as surprised as anyone this farce continued. Shortcomings aside, I kept going. I kept sacrificing—muscling my way through the debt, the firings, the layoffs, the regrets, and rejection of both professional and personal varieties. I got used to getting death threats from right-wing psychos. When I described myself, I kept it simple: "working class writer, raconteur, and enlightened dumbass" stuck. Nothing felt truer. Besides, if you tell people you're looking for nirvana, they don't really know what to do with it.

EXISTENTIAL THIRST TRAP

The only thing in this world that scares me is death (and cancer, but they go skeletal hand in hand). I realized long ago that working toward a calm mind, toward enlightenment made sense for me. The problem is that this desire represents a journey. Along with all my other fuck-ups, I keep fumbling along on the path to become awakened—continuously, daily, hourly.

I get frequent reminders that life fucking sucks. Life is suffering. No matter what, bad things will happen. We can't control everything, but we can do our best to turn into the skid. You can either become a sad sack and blame the world or use it. Pleasure is fleeting, and like a hangover surging through my body and mind, my spirit is affected too. When I feel like shit the next day, that's a price that comes with admission. Nothing, even a good time, lasts.

Knowing this is one thing. Minding it, another. I found places and people that opened up my world view, usually when I least expected it. Like, when I got into hardcore, everything changed because of the music and the culture that went with it. I'd never seen anything like this before: people screaming along, dead set on connecting with the universe one lyric at a time. This hardcore thing, the people swinging their arms like they were attacked by a swarm of killer bees, the heckling between songs, and people climbing all over one another to say their piece—I was about that life immediately. The air felt different, like the people weren't there for a collective experience of a show but something else. Communion. Transcendence. Nirvana.

Bear in mind, this was novel to me. I was a fuck up from the south side of Chicago, where I was born into a homophobic and racist culture. I never heard of anything different. In the hardcore scene, I dove into championing outside beliefs that supported a strong community of equality. Vegetarianism, racial justice, gay rights, religion—kids my age had tables set up at shows and would offer me information to work on myself. I've said and done a lot of fucked up things in my life. I'm no schoolboy. I credit hardcore as the great salve, and my one truth is that that music created me, it gave me purpose, and it showed me I could be better. Being a dumb working-class hick wasn't cool. I didn't want to stay in that old self. I wanted to grow, and hardcore gave me a way to try it. The music, people, and moment in time showed up just when I needed them, as all my personal challenges built up to something I didn't know how to vocalize.

Religion has always been hard for me. I've never been able to give myself over to the Christian church. Everyone I came up with was a broken mirror Catholic. They went to mass when someone was married, dead, or on Christmas. No one put stock into the practice but still claimed the gang. When I started to go to more shows, I gained the courage to look at those tables with the free zines, the books, and the records by bands who had a specific message rather than "fuck, drink, and die." What I got was something no one in my perimeter was talking about: Krishna and Buddhism. I started listening to bands who spoke about their spirituality, about their paths toward enlightenment. It felt earnest instead of an obligation. It reached me.

The American culture pretends we're vested in the word of Christ, but really, we'd rather be spending Sunday mornings watching the Drew Brees thread the needle into double coverage against the Falcons. Despite the laws and purpose of the church to spread good deeds, it always felt forced. For a "Christian Nation," America isn't very Christ-like. We have a national desire for more stuff, constant war. We love to see blood spill for no reason. Taking the last chicken bone for ourselves is bred into our psyches as a fundamental right rather than a reviewable offense for gluttony. Mega churches exist. High-rises sit half full because people can't afford the cost of a private pool, while countless scores stand in breadlines and hope for a cot. The

EXISTENTIAL THIRST TRAP

system has always made my skin crawl. Calling it out made me feel like at least my failures weren't for nothing. I wasn't a victim of the system, but I saw how I was taking part in it and decided to change my views.

I'm a firm believer in worshiping whatever gets you through the night. A lot of what I heard, before hardcore, simply wasn't for me. By the time I was looking at girls with hungry eyes, the jive that priests were talking rolled right off my back. I'm too logical. I want discussion, life lessons, context, and compassion. Bible study, in comparison, seemed meaningless—running your finger over a page of printed lines and hoping to impress the neighbor you'd love to give the high hard one.

Buddhism is the foundation that's made the most sense to me. My perpetual dumbass understanding of it is that its fundamentals are about continual growth. The goal is learning who you are, what your path looks like, and investing back into your whole for dharma—not because you're working toward this karmic points system but rather to spread love and compassion instead of adding another skull to the pile. Krishna has always given me similar respect for how they see life. I think the world would be a better place if more of us had the ability to look at ourselves and ask, "But what if I'm wrong?"

I'm wrong a lot, so I'm down with that. I accepted long ago that happiness is a dragon we chase. Appreciating life while we have it, that's a spiritual practice. It's essential to see the world as it is: a fucked-up but beautiful place. We're a complex, broken species, but by embracing the flaws and seeing the cracks in the veneer, it's easier to find small joys and love them, if for only a moment.

I will say, it was a lot easier to be detached and existential before I became a father. My life got complicated when I realized how much I wanted to be a constant north star for my two boys. Guiding them is my greatest priority because the world can always use more good humans. My other two crosses to bear are that this is what I do, I write. I can't do anything else. I have no interest in anything else, and the thought of *not* doing this is inconceivable. The other part that swirls everything up like a disco volante cocktail is that I'm an obsessively curious person who wants to know a little bit about everyone but also about the world I exist within. I left home to chase being a writer, but I also left because I understand that this life, right now, is the only version of Robert Dean in this dimension. How do you care without caring too much? How do you decide to be yourself knowing that your "self" will change hundreds of times in your time on Earth?

While Buddhism teaches us that reincarnation happens continually, as we work towards enlightenment through multiple incarnations, I'm pretty fucking aware of my mortality. It keeps me on my toes. I'm not saying I understand the complexities of life after death, because I don't. Who the fuck knows what happens when the lights flicker out?

With that said, I'm not a gambler. I prefer to hedge my bets. It seems to me that the best thing you can do is make sure your time alive is spent wisely. Being miserable and stuck in some garbage life isn't a shoe I want to wear. How many people do you know are fucking someone they hate, rolling over in the morning and being like, "yuck, look at this asshole"? Same goes for being trapped in a job that blows. Both make my teeth hurt. I'll take getting fired over dealing with an asshole boss. I've worked for that guy, and he sucks.

I just think that life shouldn't be this punishment of obligation. Do you have to stick something out? Probably not. I'm not saying to split on your kids, deadbeats. What I am saying is that there will always be cars that need a tune-up, but it doesn't mean you need to be the one turning the wrench.

My mission is to document the good, the bad, and gain

EXISTENTIAL THIRST TRAP

sagacity. My fear of death and thirst for knowledge siphons a placid suburban life away from me. Some folks relish the notion of their own little "slice of paradise," featuring a life with an expensive car they can't afford, coupled with an annual, all-inclusive vacation to somewhere Journey's "Don't Stop Believin'" is forced onto listeners by the hour. It's my idea of hell: endless mimosas and overflowing plates of loaded nachos served by people miserable in their polyester uniforms.

The karmic problem is no one wants anyone else's experience, just a platinum card lifestyle. Which is too fucking bad. This life is full of surprises, teachable moments, food crackling over a griddle, and places where the people don't speak your language. The same sun that sets across the Sydney opera house also tickles the swaying wheat in French fields, but most folks never look past the backyard fence line. So much hell.

My slow descent toward the grave makes me long for nights in seedy bars. On a good run, I hear bad jokes from the locals and share secrets with those older and wiser. We grow more compassionate by seeing life through the lens of strangers and enemies, lovers and friends alike. We cannot judge from the mountain unless we've attempted to get there, but one must have a curious mind to begin the path. When I realized the road to enlightenment was my way, life's habit of kicking me in the nuts with baseball cleats made a lot more sense.

When I got divorced, I made a promise to myself to get back into the shadowy corners of what I believed in. I had to look inward again. Getting married and having kids, I'd lost a slice of who I was. I lost that practice from the hardcore pits. Not taking Buddhism as seriously as I once had, I couldn't ever do that again. My struggle is eternal, but that's the path. I needed to find what was in myself so I could shed it.

At the end of the day, the picket fence life isn't for me.

ROBERT DEAN

Even when I tried to make it work, I was always aware I was wearing a costume. Now that it's behind me, I'm okay knowing that kind of life wasn't a fit. Nothing lasts forever, including me. Knowing that my path winds and curves, I roam the earth moving from one experience to another. It is just what I do. Divorce taught me that I no longer place value on time spent together but rather impact. The way I see it, I didn't waste almost a decade with someone. I learned about myself, what I needed out of life, and what I wanted for my eternity. I don't blame her for falling out of love with me. I'm a circus, and I know it.

As the hands of time move toward infinity, there are small towns, little old ladies, books, mom-and-pop joints, and stories to write that I haven't discovered yet. If I'm slouching toward nirvana, knowing I need to drown in all of these things is what gives me joy, I might as well love it—only for a moment, anyhow. I did end up going back to Jameson. Don't ask me. I just work here.

WORKING CLASS JOE

I WAS STANDING on a street corner in Chicago with my friend Marc. We were in Canaryville, my familial turf on the South Side. Marc is from the neighborhood, which is an ironclad Irish working-class stronghold. Everyone's married to someone else's cousin, and if you're imported, they'll ask you where home is without missing a beat. Whenever I find myself in a bar in Canaryville, I'm immediately asked where I'm from. As always, I have to explain I was born there and lived there as a kid. I moved away, but all of my family is still there. And once they get my last name, it's immediately met with, "Oh! You're the writer!"

Every. Single. Time.

Marc and I were making plans to get together later that evening, on my side of town. At the time, I was living on the northside in Wicker Park, which was an artist's neighborhood with cool bars and late-night coffee shops and a killer used spot, Myopic Books.

A friend of Marc's walked past. Judging by his scuffed work boots, along with the wear and tear of the breast pocket where he kept his smokes, he was a union guy. Probably a bricklayer, pipefitter, or maybe a millwright. History evades me on the actual nature of his gig. We caught up about Pearl Jam's first two records; he was lucky enough to catch Nirvana at the Aragon Ballroom back in 1993 (a show that I fucked myself out of with bad behavior). But, somehow, the conversation touched on Chris Farley, who'd recently passed away. The subject carried weight for this guy.

"Man, I remember that day like it was yesterday. I really loved that dude. He was my favorite on *Saturday Night Live*. I called my boss when I heard it on the radio. I took the rest of the day off. I went to the store and grabbed a six pack and drove to the lake alone. I sat there and thought about him."

Almost twenty years later, I still think about this conversation.

PLAGUED MIND

I'M GONNA DIE. *I'm gonna die. I'm gonna die. I'm gonna die.* This violent song is my head's private mantra. I've been dealing with it for years. It never gets easier.

What's a panic attack like? Every breath is a prayer, trying to calm your brain down. Every extremity tingles with small bites of lightning. Your heart feels like it'll explode, slamming inside the skeletal cage. Ask someone to take your pulse, and they'll tell you that you seem normal, but your hot flashes come in waves that could melt a leather seat in the summer. The words tumble out of your mouth. Sometimes they're clear. Most of the time, they're twisted, a dialect of anguish.

Asking for help is hard. Explaining what's happening is harder. Dizziness comes next. Trying to make decisions other than stopping everything makes no sense. Get out of the car wherever you're at. It's time to take a walk. You can't stop moving. You need air. You need white noise. You need the outside world. You need to breathe. Remember the meditation breathing techniques: long noseful of air in for six seconds, hold for six seconds, exhale for six seconds. Repeat till human. If you sit still, your heart will combust. If you stop moving, you'll black out. If you black out, you'll never wake up.

I know the signs. I know when my body is about to go haywire. My last big one, I was driving down the access road along the highway, the flashes of neon promoting burger joints and oil changes turning blurrier with each mile. My head tangled into a knot. I got dizzier and dizzier. I knew what was coming but didn't want to believe it. It'd been at least a year since I'd had a panic attack. I was with the woman I'd been seeing; we were on our way to get tacos. We weren't fighting. Nothing was weird. Well, the world was, but we weren't.

Everything hit me all at once. The election was the night before. I'd drunk almost a bottle of Jameson to quell the anxiety I felt as we waited to see the results, America's fate. I couldn't handle another four years of Donald Trump. 2020 had worked over my psyche like a heavyweight boxer. I'd gone through a divorce. A pandemic. I lost my job. I felt like my writing flatlined. I was phoning it in for this relationship. I gained weight. I couldn't sleep. I felt like I was going to die from something new daily. My kids were always on my mind. My best friend was moving away. Everything attacked my senses like a hungry Bengal tiger. The fear was its feast.

My mom has anxiety. So do my brothers. This disease comes with our blood. They take pills for it. They can live life through their particular chemical haze. I can't. My body and mind reject drugs, so I drown myself in CBD. We come from the Irish people. These folks helped build America—they lived hand to mouth for generations. We're hard, from a stock of people built to last, and here I was, walking off an anxiety attack on a sidewalk in Texas, apologizing for how my brain misfires.

Maybe the panic is part of me, or maybe I'm the thing that's out of joint. I come from ancestors who worked themselves into the grave. I don't know their names. I just get pieces of their animalistic coding. DNA isn't fair. I am not in fight or flight. I am not in danger. I'm a writer. I wear comfortable shoes. I have never had to work a forklift like my father. Never took an icepick to the hip like my great-grandfather. And yet my brain punishes me for thinking,

EXISTENTIAL THIRST TRAP

for feeling, for living. I wonder if my people from long ago ever felt like this, or were they too fucking tired? I don't know, but I'd trade a stab wound for a stable mind.

ANXIETY, MY EX-WIFE, AND ME

I wrote this piece for Fatherly *during a personal disaster. I felt the bricks giving way underneath me at a dreamlike pace. Anxiety was beating my organs and brain into submission. I was miserable professionally. I liked freelancing, but our bills were stacking up. I remember that when I was writing this, I wanted so badly for my ex to hold the story close to her chest. This essay was meant as an outpouring of love, proof that I did appreciate her, even when we weren't on the same page. I was doing my best, but things were slipping through my fingers at every turn. I wrote this because I wanted to give her something that I might have not said in person. I did the thing I do best, made money from it, and did it in her name.*

"QUIT FREAKING OUT," my wife, Sarah, said, stirring a steaming pot of hippie mac & cheese. "We'll be okay. You're not a terrible dad, and you're a good husband. The world isn't ending. We'll find a way, we always do."

She dropped the spoon when I kept pacing and grabbed me by the shirt, offering a quick squeeze before pushing me away—I was dripping wet and nasty.

I'd just come in the house after walking off an anxiety attack to find our two-year-old, Luke, sitting on the couch munching goldfish crackers and watching *Hey Duggee*.

EXISTENTIAL THIRST TRAP

Meanwhile, our five-year-old scallywag, Jackson, streamed Halloween videos on our iPad. The two were oblivious to my stormy attitude. I was stuck in a mental state somewhere between *my heart is going to explode* and *should I walk straight into traffic*.

"I never expected it to be this hard," I said to my family, feeling like a dripping wax figure in the Texas heat. "I'm sorry I let you and the boys down."

Over the past few weeks, a whole lot of terrible rained down upon us. Our dog Gracie kicked the bucket. The next day, I rolled into work clutching my still-warm vegetarian banh mi and was greeted with a pink slip. They didn't need a writer on staff anymore, so I was back in the unemployment line. By Tuesday afternoon, I was stuck explaining to Sarah how, once again, I was out of a job. I was most definitely not living my best life.

There were a few close calls. After applying for a bazillion jobs, I thought I finally had a life-changing one in the bag. I was making plans for a last-minute family trip to Disney World and getting ready to finally put in new floors when *whoops*, the dreaded "thanks, but no thanks" call came. They said "I'd get bored with the job," which was one that would have dramatically changed our lives. The pay was insane. I wouldn't know, firsthand. The panic rushed up, nipping at me with its rancid jaws. Then, as now, I only had one option: walk it off. Far and hard. Until I was too tired to care anymore. Each time was the same.

"I gotta get out of here or I'm gonna explode," I would tell her as she looked at me and sighed. "I didn't get that job," I barely squeaked out, then slipped on my knock-off Ray Bans, slid my feet into my Vans, and split.

In my panic attacks, everything bubbles up inside. All of the terrible things I feel about myself and my place in the world come roaring back. Despite trying my hardest to be a competent father and a good husband, I have to live every day with severe anxiety, plus some depression sprinkled in for good measure. Anxiety and me, we're locked in a knife fight. One of us might catch a lick and win a round, but the battle never stops. There are hot flashes, GERD, panic attacks, bounding pulse, and major mood swings. Yes, I'm a positive joy.

While the kids had no idea Daddy has a few screws loose, Sarah did. She took the heat. Now, I would fight a ravenous Siberian tiger for my wife. I adore her. I am not my anxiety. But I get moody and never say *I'm sorry* fast enough. In my head, I'm processing how I was just an asshole and figuring out how I can make it up. I want to apologize, but for some reason, I can't. I know I've hit the wife lottery jackpot—she is a badass nurse who saves lives every day—but all the same, the struggle is real.

Once my anxiety has peaked and I'm coming back to my right mind, I focus on my blessings. Sarah is a tireless mother and an immovable partner. She is the kind of woman who, after seven years, a house note, a dead dog, and a 2001 Mazda Protege that barely runs, still makes my heart thunder when I see her come in for a kiss. On my walk back to our house that particular evening, my mind kept returning to thoughts about how I don't want us to struggle. I want her to look at our bank account and not worry about whether we should skip our fancy night out. I fantasy-shop for things all the time. I want her to be able to buy stuff she loves, like cute rockabilly dresses. But the reality is she's stuck with a TV that's hard to watch in the dark because it has a weird blue streak running across it.

After washing the nasty off with a cold shower, I came back to the kitchen to find Sarah taking bites from a small bowl of leftover noodles.

"I believe in you," she said. "I always have. And I always will."

I listened to her voice: stern but ultimately loving. Living with severe anxiety sucks, but we're here for our boys, and we love each other—even if Sarah sometimes

EXISTENTIAL THIRST TRAP

feels like she wants to kill me. Thankfully, she's more level-headed than most. But, if there's one truth I do know, it's this: for all of my ticks and flaws, there's no one I'd rather silently freak out in bed next to than Sarah, Siberian tiger and all.

That's how it was, but not how it is. With the marriage long over, I can look at what I was doing with clarity. I meant what I said about her, yes. It was also a last-ditch effort to reignite sparks between us. I'm glad we're co-parents rather than married. We're better this way. It makes sense. We're two different people, and we don't deserve to be miserable, separately or together. Reading this over, I can see the pain and desperation in my words, the way I framed the narrative—how much I wanted her to see me through the anxiety, that I adored her, even at our worst.

This was a love letter to the void. What came spiraling out was different than I expected, but sometimes that broken clock of love needs to be put out in the trash. Better hands will repair it and give hearts a better home. At the very least, I have solid proof I loved her. I remember everything. And see? I wrote it down.

LITTLE BASTARD

Dear Kid,

I'm sorry I don't remember your name. You might remember mine. I want you to know I think about you. All the time.

Where we grew up on the South Side of Chicago, you had to be bulletproof. Black people didn't walk on *that* side of the viaduct. Gay people were relegated to the dens of iniquity on the North Side. Where we grew up, dudes named Sullivan drank Miller Lite longnecks and listened to Led Zeppelin, catcalled the girls from down the block, and smoked cheap reefer. Even on the quiet streets.

You and me, we did typical stupid kid stuff. We played "games" like Smear the Queer—if you had the football, everyone else had to beat the crap out of you before you made it to the goal line. There was a dude in my grade everyone called "Pat the Fag" when he wasn't around. Whether he was gay or not didn't matter; we thought he was soft. If you didn't have hard hands or an iron will, you weren't going that far down, where the streets numbered in the 100s.

I remember meeting you on the corner near my mom's house. My friend Brian from down the street knew your name. I remember him picking on you. And I remember tormenting you right along with Brian because *he* was tough. His dad used to kick the snot out of him for not

EXISTENTIAL THIRST TRAP

being hard enough every day, and I didn't want to seem weak around a guy like that. I joined in as we chased you, screaming, "Get the homo!"

No one in the neighborhood cared. It was business as usual.

I remember how we cornered you by a wooden fence. You pleaded for help, and no one came. Anybody listening probably tried to tell themselves we were "playing." We weren't.

When you slipped from our grip, you ran like hell. We didn't chase. We felt like we saved the world from one more sissy. I was a popular kid—no arrest record—who found joy listening to Megadeth tapes and eating cheese pizza. Not a deep thinker. Not big on empathy. This was a moment of peer pressure, ignorance, and weakness, engineered by two blond fifth-graders in baggy Metallica shirts, thinking they were the coolest jerks on skateboard wheels.

Decades have passed, and even now, I'll lie in bed remembering how I felt like someone else after we attacked you. I felt gross. Empty. All this from a guy who takes it personally when someone doesn't like *me*. Chances are you could have used a friend in our world.

I was 9 or 10. I grew up. I found different friends. I discovered punk rock and, eventually, hardcore, which taught me about people, life, politics, and community. I listened when Kurt Cobain preached tolerance.

That experience, though, lives in my bone marrow, and I have to own the shame. I have so many beautiful gay and trans friends now that it turns my stomach to know how ugly I was as a boy. The last time I brought it up was in San Francisco, on the last day of Pride, of all places. I drunk-cried about what I'd done on the way to a gay bar with my friend Will—Will, whose homophobic father hated him so much Will killed himself over it. Don't tell me these acts don't have consequences. These words leave a mark that is hard to wash off.

ROBERT DEAN

As a straight white guy, I need to be honest about my mistakes—and to stand taller as an ally during an ugly time. I'm a dad now, in charge of two little boys. I'll never teach them anything but love, openness, and kindness. I'm proud of where I'm from; I love the South Side. But I want my boys to experience life alongside all their friends, no matter their color, religion, or who they want to kiss. They're growing faster every day. They might be gay, bi, or trans. I just hope their hearts will be free.

Kid, I hope whatever life you slid into is a good one. I wish I could make up for the past. All I can do is work on the future, beginning with my own sons. And I can say to straight white men like me—with the privileges that identity brings us—that we're all capable of doing ugly things. In the post-Brett Kavanaugh world, we can't bury the past. We need to meet it head-on. I can't call myself an ally today without admitting I've been ugly too. For you, and for everyone who's ever been mistreated, screamed at, or felt small in a big room, I'm sorry.

Kid, I wish I knew your name. This is the best way I have to tell you I'm eternally sorry. I'm sorry for the disrespect, and I'm sorry I didn't stand up for you. I hope you can hear my apology.

Sincerely,

Bobby

(NB. Since the publication, the power of the Internet led me to this guy. I apologized to him. He didn't remember me.)

PLAN B

IN 1989, I was eight. I don't remember what grade I was in, but my class had to dress up like a person from history and give a speech. My contemporaries picked Jack Kennedy, Neil Armstrong, Susan B. Anthony, Martin Luther King. I picked Genghis Khan.

Having just seen *Bill and Ted's Excellent Adventure*, I thought the guy was cool. I mean, he knocked the head off a mannequin on a skateboard with a baseball bat. Little Bobby borrowed Grandpa's plastic safari hat, the kind that 1930s Hollywood explorers wore. I constructed a costume of robes and a spear. I even had a fake goatee. My classmates gave speeches about the first man to walk on the moon or what it was like to draw Mickey Mouse. I talked about Mongol raids and how Genghis Khan sired countless kids and absolutely murdered motherfuckers. The kid that went after me pretended to be Henry Ford. His talk on the Model-T fell flat. It's a hard act to follow: the screaming kid brandishing a stabbing weapon.

This is just who I am.

I've seen my name in print, and I've had my successes. I've had strangers both say nice things and tell me explicitly how much of a piece of shit I am. It's a mixed bag.

Most of my friends had plans, or at least ideas. I've had one thing I chase: this nonsense. It's hard looking back on life at certain times, especially when your bank account is god damned *ugly*.

Being a writer is not sexy. It's not fun. It's a perfunction of who you are as a person. It's a sickness you can't kick. But most of all, it's a hard life to attach yourself to because it ain't easy. If you're considering tempting the fates to write, just know hopes and dreams aren't protected. They're not a secret kept in the center of a fist. Instead, they're ripped out of your claws.

I've never had a Plan B. My mind does not function as an average adult's. I don't know how to make a secondary plan. Writing is the only thing I've cared about since I was seventeen years old. I'm going on forty. After bouts of unemployment, freelancing, varying degrees of success, and a divorce, the last couple decades feel like a war movie. "Smoke 'em if ya got 'em" is applicable. I have no idea what I'm doing. I've been winging it for twenty years and falling upward.

Doing this for a living or a hobby is like fighting a grizzly with a pillow. Some days, you might get that son of a bitch right on the snout. Most of the time, though, it's still a bear. A snarling beast with big-ass paws that slap the life out of you. You will never be above the art. This ain't rock and roll. The groupies won't be waiting alongside the podium.

Fixing AC units, pouring a strong whiskey, making things with your hands—those are *jobs*. Swinging the hammer, building up the world one block at a time, that's how you survive the seasons, the depressions, the politics of the world. I scribble stories about pipelines and a president who deserved a jail cell and a shaved head, to see his clown makeup wiped away. I write about petty criminals, cover the news, and wax like a poetic-ass blowhard any chance I get. These things create a life worth living. However, it's not exactly recession friendly.

It comes with its own problems of the interior variety too. For example, I wake up every morning ready to knife fight the world. All of the emotions that dance inside me,

EXISTENTIAL THIRST TRAP

whether it be my anxiety or depression. I have people in my head that I still want to prove a point to years later. I stay angry at life, not because I've been dealt a bad hand but because it's my nature to attack the problem. I'm not talented, I'm tenacious. Sticking around is the longest game, just wearing people down with my bullshit.

If I never learned how to copywrite, I'd still be in the bar. I'd be tap dancing for tourists on Bourbon Street. I'd be hollering for people to line dance. Every day I worked in the French Quarter, a little bit of my soul's hourglass sand slipped to the bottom. Learning to write professionally opened up the lane for escape from deep within my own woods.

The gig teaches you to get hard. Editors strip away hubris. No matter how good you get or whatever you achieve, there's always a white-haired kung fu master, complete with a long beard, ready and willing to chop you down to size. They make your soul *mean* because they have to, otherwise you can't relate, and if you can't relate, you're obsolete. You have to accept the hard parts that come with the release of each page. It's hard to make the words do their job. It's hard to be useful when you need to string together logic or a fairytale.

This is a cautionary tale. Writing is the shittiest of all of the choices. It's like spinning the wheel of poverty and landing on the sparkly whammy with a pack of smokes and a bottle of Jameson taped on it. Accept it for what it is, Bukowski.

When I moved to New Orleans, I had all my stuff in my car and $300 to my name. I wanted to make it work like Burroughs, Tennessee Williams, and all of the other writers who did time down at "the bottom of the map," as Lil Wayne says. When I left Chicago, it was with one singular goal: to do this thing I love. I worked in bars, and I hustled my way through a chaotic five years. I took mental and emotional beatdowns, drank the whiskey, had the long nights, and scribbled down notes along the way.

ROBERT DEAN

I hated every minute of high school outside of English, writing, and trades classes, where I learned how to paint a house. High school didn't work as a system for teaching me. They wanted us to be model citizens. They wanted us to *want* to work in the banks or swing a hammer. If you ask me, I'm a terrible adult. Sure, I've got kids and try to impart life lessons like Red Foreman or Homer Simpson, but I'm flying blind. I have no idea what I'm doing. Ever.

By the time I was a junior, I didn't care about school, my classmates, or most of my teachers. It was all an illusion. They were teaching us that if you worked hard, you, too, could raise a family and have a house. Seeing photos of my married-and-happy friends, with their white fences and tasteful backsplashes, I'm glad they got what they wanted. That life doesn't appeal to me but acts as a constant reminder of the choices I've made. I'm comfortable in my own skin, I do what I love for a living, but there's never a safety net. This tightrope will kill me if I fall.

Nearing forty two, the idea of no Plan B sounds scarier every day. Sometimes, I feel like the future dances on the blade of a knife. I am well aware of how exhausting I sound. I have to live with me. I might be a lot of things, but I'm definitely no pony ride.

On days when the world gets heavy and a long, hot shower can't shake the demons away, there's always the fantasy of giving it up and bum-rushing the void. That might be nice—realizing you weren't that good, nothing you said was that special, and you are mediocre despite your best efforts. What do you do when you finally accept things like this? Keep pounding, I guess.

There's a fantasy I have where I can let go, finally stop chasing success and breathe without a second thought of this work, this life. Some days, sliding into the gutter seems real nice. For a while, I've been thinking about winding up in a cheap motel in Vietnam. The food's good. I don't mind

EXISTENTIAL THIRST TRAP

the heat. I stay there for years, minding my business, not writing a word. The cleaning lady finds me in my own filth. Two boxers pummel one another on a silent television while the world that never was reflects off my corneas. It gets dark here, but I have to keep going. There is no Plan B. No matter how tempting the void is, it can't know my name.

ONE GRAY HAIR AT A TIME

I'M SLOUCHING TOWARD IRRELEVANCE. No one gives a shit about what I like doing or where I want to go. I buy books written by dead French philosophers and newspaper journalists from the 1950s. I routinely research who's got the best vegetarian food in every town. I hunt down Bad Brains records and documentaries on octopuses. I can sit and stare at the *Addams Family*, westerns, and *Twilight Zone* in perfect harmony all day and never once wish a frame was in color. These decidedly uncool hobbies, along with the gray stripes in my beard, signify my drift. Any day now, I'll be wandering like a ghost. More than once, I've felt like those movie scenes where the dude stands still dramatically, looking into the camera, while life moves at a blurred pace.

Our language is continually evolving, but that's the nature of the American experience. We don't say "boffo" or "the bee's knees" any longer, but we sure as hell know what "WAP" means. Do you know what word I do like? *Drip*. That shit works. It's impactful, and it doesn't take a dummy to figure it out. It kills because of the immediacy and the ability to make irony cool at the same time. *Respect the drip*. Fuck yes, we all do.

Becoming a lame old dude has its perks. You can pick up the bar tab when someone's had a garbage day. You know where the best burger is in town because you're way fatter. You've got multiple pairs of shoes dedicated to

EXISTENTIAL THIRST TRAP

comfort, not style. You have a favorite talk radio host. And sometimes, staying in sounds a whole lot better than being around loud people. It's been a blessing to know when you don't want to do something and are emotionally capable of telling your posse, "Thanks, but no thanks. I'll meet you at the bar later." That shit is powerful.

I don't give a fuck what's going on, but I wonder about what's next for us culturally. Will we dive deeper into memes or videos of simple pleasures? People wanted more than bite-sized information. But our attention spans are getting shorter. We crave long-form content with podcasts, binge watches, and sometimes books. How does the divide work?

A while back, I took an Amtrak train from Austin to Chicago. Talk about a cultural exchange of what the fuck is going on in the world. I got drunk in the middle of the night, and an old man wanted to fight me for trying to be friendly to a stripper who'd just gotten out of jail and was catching the next leg of her trip. He was convinced *they* were going to screw in the cheap seats down below deck. How they would work this out, I had no idea. I sprung for a tiny private room with a shitty bed and a lockable door. I met strangers from across the country and a lovely couple from Belgium. Women danced to Sam Cooke as they served meals to the first-class passengers, who got progressively meaner from St. Louis to Chicago.

It was a minor tutorial about how we interact with folks on a day-to-day basis. What will 2020 equate to for us as a whole, I wonder. What will it mean in hindsight? When we're allowed out of our crypts at full capacity, will we be friendlier and appreciative to be with people, or will we be bigger assholes in a post-Trump world?

It's essential to grab a seat at life's table and look out the glass ceiling, past the towns with one stoplight or where their politics don't look like mine. Life at an old man's pace is pretty fucking good. I might keep it up. Like, when we can get back out there, can we just put the phones down? Can we maybe wait a little bit and offer a recap a few hours later? In a post-pandemic world, sitting at the park with friends and a few beers sounds a lot better than filming every waking second in hopes someone hits a heart button for minor validation.

The only guarantee life offers is that if you stick around, you're gonna be old. Honestly, it's working for me. Give it a try sometime. Accept you're not cool, as I have accepted it. Go gently into the night. Love your hobbies, your quirks that keep you unfuckable. Really, they're what makes us who we are, one episode of *the Munsters* at a time.

PERSONALIZED

REGRET COMES EASY. The stinger takes a little longer to dig out, but most times, I leave it in. I like to remind myself I'm human. The past can seem intoxicating, but let those sleeping dogs lie. There is only forward. There is only tomorrow. Yesterday is dead and gone. There is no time travel, and the bones of the past make up our collective history.

Sometimes, the past is packaged in our minds as the greatest steak with all of the fixin's; but in the reality we know is true, it's a bite into a cheap, lifeless fast-food burger, consumed on a plastic bench in a joint where everyone is locked in shared misery. The meat tastes its color: gray.

Sometimes regret comes in a bottle. The mistakes are poured out one by one. Salvation doesn't come from getting fucked up, it's a band-aid for the moment. You can play kick-the-can-down-the-road with your darkest feelings, but when the streetlights run out, reality will be right there with its palm open, ready for payment and waiting for you.

I dwell on the graveyards of past mistakes only to tell myself there's always redemption and there are no timelines. There are, and there aren't. Who knows anymore.

I'll wonder what the fuck I've been doing all these years. Whose demons have I been boxing with? Are they mine, or are they everyone else's? Was it worth it?

All I know is the mantra etched into my heart: destroy the thing in your heart that makes you weep, but love it too.

SOME DISASTER

MY FRIEND LYNETTE is mad at me. Again. We were supposed to hang out on her birthday. We were supposed to hang out and do something else on another day too. And I forgot about that. She's a planner and I am not. I've adopted this whole "live by the seat of your pants" thing, and it works for me. I'm not a space case; if we mention going shopping for new Vans next week, I might remember, I might not. It's all or nothing in that black hole up there.

If you need me when there's trouble, I'll be there. I'll text on your birthday, but

I don't understand the hamster maze that is my brain. If someone wants to kick it, I'm down. I like people, I'm an extrovert, but I'm also an everyday psychopath. If it's not written down or in a Google calendar or on a slip of paper I keep in my pocket, forget it. If I don't make a reminder a week out and then two days out, it'll go straight through the ether. I've had a standing appointment every Monday with my chiropractor, and every Monday, I forget about it. Minutes before I'm supposed to show up, he'll ask if a different time is better and I'll be like, "oh fuck!" and I'll scarf down the taco I'm working on and jet over to his place.

About once a week, someone will text me, "Hey, how are you?" and I'll dive into the conversation straightaway. I genuinely give a shit about your day. *How's your dad?*

EXISTENTIAL THIRST TRAP

Did his surgery go okay? Please tell me everything because I care. Do I remember to text first? Nope. (The sole exception is my mother, whom I have a longstanding every-other-day conversation with.)

It's not personal. A lot is going on up there. There's the anxiety and depression thing, and that I'm never just sitting around waiting for the phone to ring. I quit social media because I want fewer interactions that distract from me being sane. I go for hours-long walks, listening to the world at night, counting my steps, watching the branches of trees dance in a slight breeze. These movements are mantras toward a quiet mind. I hate phones. I understand we need them to keep up in today's world, but I prefer to spend my time staring into the void, searching for that hit of dopamine.

My brothers and my mom joke about my aloofness. Once, my mom called me while she and my brothers and their wives were hanging out. Since I live across the country, I check in sometimes, but not daily.

"Hey, your brother says you never call him. Call him right now to tell you love him."

She snickered. She'd been hitting the Miller Lite.

"I don't want to call him. Please don't make me do this."

"Come on. It'll be funny."

"To tell him I love him?"

"And tell him you're thinking about him!"

I groaned. I hate doing stupid human tricks. When I rang my brother, he was genuinely surprised. When he answered, I could hear it in his voice, like the universe had connected the dots for a moment.

"Mom made me do it."

"See! I knew it! You *never* call to check in!"

That's one reason the lockdown sucked for me: I'm a social person. The bar is my home away from home. I love cutting up with strangers, grabbing food from new spots, hitting as many shows as possible. I like the random interactions that life provides on the hour. If you follow the zodiac signs, I'm a Leo, and apparently, we need to be the center of attention. I suggest you let *that* idea marinate.

Being stuck inside did a number on my brain. (One positive thing about the coronavirus, though, is that I did buy a bidet, and what the fuck was I doing before? Jesus, wiping your ass is shitting like a peasant.) When they said the lockdown was only going to be for a few weeks, I treated it like one extended drunk sleepover. I live with my best friend post-divorce, and in the beginning, I made extravagant meals while we binge drank every day, sleeping till three or four in the afternoon. We cycled through on endless repeat till it wasn't fun anymore. And, being an extrovert, the lack of new people drained me.

Once things opened back up in Texas, I started traveling around the state, working from rentals to get some alone time. It gave me a chance to feel a sense of adventure, hit a new town, and spend time in my favorite Texas city—Galveston. I've grown up around concrete my whole life. When I hear the music of the ocean, something becomes whole again. Standing on the seawall, looking out at the endless expanse of water, reminds me how small and insignificant I am to the universe. It acts as a salve and quiets my overloaded brain for an hour or two.

Galveston *isn't* cool, which is what I enjoy about it. To the Houston locals an hour north, the town is a dated, dirty, and unwelcoming little island. Perfect. It doesn't offer lavish opportunities to act like a douche, with over-priced bottle service while overflowing with Instagrammable spots. Instead, Galveston is quiet. The tourists stroll in from cruise ships every few days, and the seawall is packed on the weekends during the warm weather, but once the beach is out of the equation and the ships have slowed down, it's all locals. And those locals don't give a single fuck about what's happening on "the mainland."

EXISTENTIAL THIRST TRAP

There's a mojo about Galveston. It's quiet and loud at the same time. It dances between controlled chaos but also never demands anything further than your ability to shut the fuck up about "fun" once you're schooled in the local code. Whatever rules Austin has for public engagement, Galveston long eschewed them. They consider themselves a part of Texas on a technicality, connected by name only. When things were locked down with specific rules, the "free state of Galveston" figured it out on a case-by-case basis. Floating from the dives throughout downtown and on The Strand, I felt like myself. I used my getaways to keep myself emotionally balanced. I needed something to look forward to, even if I was doing the same things I always do but in a new place.

And then, as if 2020 couldn't get any worse, July happened. The long, black forever came crashing down on me. I couldn't get out of bed. All of my writing sounded like spit from the cages on death row. I wasn't reading like normal. I wasn't hitting the bottle, really, either. I wasn't doing much of anything but trying to stay employed. Ironically, I was hired to work on an e-book about employee mental health. Looking back, it was one long call for help. The structure was broken; entire passages read like they were written at gunpoint. Still, I worked my way through the bleakness inside of me spilled on the page. When I wasn't faking it for work, I couldn't get out of bed. If I wasn't asleep, I was staring at my wall.

The lack of human interaction grated on me. The only people I'd touched for six months were my boys, and I was barely present for them. As a dad, I phoned it in. I let my kids run wild on the weekend. I had nothing to give. I couldn't parent them when I was a corpse floating through life. Whatever they wanted to watch, I didn't care. YouTube was their babysitter. I was hardly alive. The first hug I got was from a friend, and it was such a shock to my system that it felt like getting a shot in the arm.

My birthday is August 15, and for my gift to myself, I had to get the fuck out of town. I had to do something to shake the death off. I put some money aside and booked a small beach house in Galveston for six days. I took off from the day job, so I only worked on poems and essays, not corporate bullshit. My birthday present to myself was my sanity.

It was the best gift. Every morning, I woke up and got dressed for the beach. I didn't go into the water, just walked for miles along the line where the water breaks against the sand. The gulls flew overhead while children darted between the waves and their parents, sand stuck to their fists. My depression kept me company, but its grip wasn't as tight. I worked on my books and drank hot cups of CBD tea, listening to the wind break through the palms. I fed my leftover meal scraps to the birds, who scooped them up like squawking, pecking savages.

I strolled through the aisles of the used bookstore. I bought fresh shrimp off the back of the boats. It was good to watch the world drift by like the clouds. I didn't put in my headphones; I didn't speak to anyone other than an occasional hello. I existed within the landscape for those moments, observing rather than taking part. I needed those days to feel human again. I watched feral cats run along the sidewalks. For once, I wasn't thinking about being a good dad, surviving through a pandemic, living in my best friend's house, missing my dog, missing people, or feeling so alone; I let it all drift off into the waves of an unforgiving ocean. I let the whales, the sea creatures, and God sort that out. The waves crashing against the shore was the only answer I got.

When I drove back up to Austin, I felt like a screw was put back into place. It was the first time I'd seen the world with clear eyes in months. Depression is a motherfucker. The world can lose its flavor, life can seem like it's worthless, but there is a way out. Nothing wrong with

EXISTENTIAL THIRST TRAP

claiming a few days to get your mind right by staring out at the water and shutting your phone off. Hopefully, soon, Lynette will stop being mad at me. I'm doing my best with a broken brain. I'm still learning how to fix it, one mantra at a time.

KITCHEN NECROMANCY

WHEN YOU'RE A crazy person, rituals matter. Small details keep me sane, keep me grounded. Sometimes, the salt and pepper shakers *do* need to be in an exact spot, and God knows I've checked to make sure all of the doors are locked multiple times before leaving the house. If you saw my desk, it looks like the inside of my head: piles of crap from a scene straight out of hoarders. Let's say, it's a complex content management system. But the rest of the house has to be spotless because living in squalor or mess sends me off the rails. Cleaning is free therapy for me—especially in the kitchen.

Show me a sink full of dishes and get the fuck out of my way. I'll throw on Bobby Womack and drift off into a different world. I love washing dishes, working till there's no food grime left. I don't mind the drying if there's a towel nearby either. If there are stubborn bits and pieces left in the pan, don't worry, I know how to get rid of anything with a little hot water and the stove.

Got a mountain of clothes that need to be folded? I'm your huckleberry. Folding clothes, matching socks—these are silent meditations. The movements of fitting corners or putting things on hangers quiet the noise in my head. Sometimes, that noise is loud. Living with anxiety, it's like a series of television channels showing the worst possible scenarios on repeat with no breaks for commercials.

Anxiety and depression rage through my body and

EXISTENTIAL THIRST TRAP

brain 24/7. Whatever I do is an attempt to battle them, from studying Buddhism and taking long walks to trying a steady diet of CBD in all its various forms. I find the most relief in the kitchen. That's the safe place I can turn to when shit really goes off the rails. Since my early 20s, cooking has been my passion. I love being in a kitchen, sweating as I make myself whole, one dish at a time. For me, cooking isn't a hobby. It's expressing myself in a way I can't do with a brush or a pen.

I take pride in the fact that I can enter any conversation about cooking. I'm nowhere near being a master; more like a culinary Bodhisattva. I roll up with my positive intent ready to learn, accept, and grow on the continual path toward flavor. Now, I can cook just about anything. I'm perennially working on self-improvement. Cooking is no different. When I meet real line-tested kitchen pirates, I always have questions, and if they'll show me their tricks, I'll buy the shots.

Food offers a mental respite. The kitchen is a place that I can retreat into because it lives within the moment and I'm driving. Working toward a vegan curry or throwing down to impress a dinner party with ribeyes and creamed spinach, these are mantras for me. Crafting a roux demands focus and time. It gets me out of my head because when I'm cooking, I cannot allow for any thought other than *stir, stir, stir*.

Obsessing over mise en place, checking my knives, and planning a meal all require stepping away from the void. For once, I'm not obsessing about being broke or deconstructing being alone. When I'm working on a shrimp scampi, I'm not thinking about death, which usually crosses my mind at least five times a day. Instead, I'm lost in the magic of planning and executing. Making sauce is an opera. Smashing burgers in a cast iron is sexual. Who doesn't love a thick homemade alfredo? My challenge is to constantly test, to experiment—can I do this better than the last time? This is a part of mindfulness. Food is intrinsically therapeutic because of its nature. That's why when we're sad, we inhale fried chicken or a greasy slice of tavern cut Chicago-style pizza. Food reminds me of Mom and better times—and damn, if Ben and Jerry's doesn't hit the spot when shit is 100% bogus.

When I'm making scrambled eggs for a breakfast spread or working a chicken parm that requires a few different prep stations while I keep my eye on a potful of al dente noodles, it's therapy. There are all these studies that link mindful concentration to happiness. Cooking offers me that; in the kitchen, I have what researchers would call goal-oriented behavior, something I read called "behavioral activation." It keeps me on task. Cooking for my kids, friends, or a date gives me a sense of purpose and provides a useful service. Cooking is my way of showing that I care about you.

There's a beautiful necromancy about being able to look in my cupboards and fridge and whip something up through some educated alchemy. I've got no use for the microwave outside warming up butter, and I certainly don't use it for cooking. The microwave doesn't involve me in its process, and I don't like that. Give me a blue flame and get the fuck out of my way. I'll make you what you want; if I've never done it before, that's even better. Trust me, it's good for both of us. When I'm working out how to tackle an authentic French dish, I'm not worrying about what happens when I die. I'm thinking about now. This spice, this meal. This moment.

What should I make next?

LAST COURSE

I ALWAYS THOUGHT I'd meet Anthony Bourdain. As my career evolved, I was increasingly convinced we'd cross paths. I imagined that I would be one of those writers he loved. I saw us sitting together, sucking down Lone Star longnecks in a roadside diner somewhere in West Texas. Maybe we'd go on an adventure down in Melbourne just to talk about why we loved the Ramones and The Stooges. About why books matter, why writing is a hard life, not dissimilar to the pirate mentality of a line cook.

Being a writer as well as someone obsessed with the kitchen, I assumed this relationship was a natural fit— game recognizing game. He was my idol. A beacon of hope that a punk rock loser could get a win. I don't have many heroes, but Bourdain was a guy who'd battled his demons. As someone who fights depression, I thought I knew him.

My fantasies were the kind of soulmate-friendships you only see in Tarantino movies. I imagined myself with Bourdain, taking turns opining about Pam Grier flicks like *Coffy* or just how badass Michael Caine was in the original *Get Carter*. We'd order a round of Jameson and extol our love of Jim Harrison's *Legends of The Fall*. I could hear the clink of our shot glasses as we kicked off a bender of epic proportions. He'd dub me an heir to his throne. We'd exchange texts and samples of whatever we were writing. Maybe we could cross paths on the road and bond about tikka masala or Old Towne Inn in Chicago. He'd ask which was the Rolling Stones' best record, and I would reply, "Fuckin' *Exile on Mainstreet*, of course." And we'd be off to the races.

It was a good fantasy, and now, it'll forever remain only that—make-believe.

I know things because of Bourdain. I envied him, of course. He shared meals with some of humanity's most exceptional people when, in reality, he was one of the finest too. Anthony Bourdain wasn't just a host. He was the guy who snuck in the back door, leaving a crack open for the rest of us.

When people die, it rakes me over the emotional coals, challenging my sense of being and purpose. Death dares me to ask: What does it mean to live genuinely? Can I carry on someone's legacy? Whose memory affects me most profoundly?

Losing Anthony Bourdain is a knife in the gut. This one hurt. *Bad*. How could someone who realized the dream, who seemingly achieved the peak experience, burn it like a slip of paper released into the ether? I'll never know what went on inside of his head. That was Tony's choice. He faced his own version of oblivion, locked away inside his five-star French hotel room.

Folks from all over the world mused about his greatness, his likability, his genuine nature, that he was an A+ original. They weren't wrong. Every note and letter adoring his name was a statement in truth; our species is better off for getting to know him over these last two decades. People from every walk of life watched *A Cook's Tour*, *No Reservations*, and *Parts Unknown*. I'm not the only one who voyeuristically imagined myself drinking a cold beer in the jungles of Brazil or wandering on the streets of Tokyo through his adventures. I learned new things about people on the other side of the planet. I lost a lot of my preconceived notions about other cultures and

EXISTENTIAL THIRST TRAP

opened my mind. Anthony Bourdain taught me how food binds across vast differences, often representing the things we're willing to fight for (spices, sugar, chocolate, potatoes). All life centers around food, and whether you dine seated on the floor or at a table, it's an experience we all share as a people. If there's a universal truth I know, it's that food makes people better. At least, less assholes. Even if I hate another person's opinions, points of view, and guts, there is always the commonality of the meal. Anthony Bourdain tapped into that.

I tend to be a lot less mean when a medium rare steak served with a glistening plate of waffle fries is dropped in my lap. Anthony Bourdain dared me to sit at life's table, no matter how awkward the conversation, to find a solution, in spite of the gravity of the world.

Before *Kitchen Confidential*, chefs were seen as these guys with folded arms in starched white jackets and big funny hats. That show let people in on the secrets of the service industry, that everything wasn't gleaming and pristine. Bourdain pulled the curtain back with his trademark affectionate irreverence. That book changed my relationship with the food I eat. Everything was less about how a plate comes out to the table but how I was the mechanism of the environment it was centered on. Before Bourdain, I thought of the Food Network as just knives hitting the cutting board, not a real peek into the industry of service. They didn't know what to do with Anthony Bourdain. Instead of embracing his weirdness, they laid their chips on safe programming. Oops. After just one season, *A Cook's Tour* was pulled. To the Travel Channel went Bourdain, and the beginnings of an empire were created.

Despite food being the pulse of *No Reservations* and *Parts Unknown*, the people he featured are what made the body of work shine. He taught how to appreciate the far corners of the world—how the people in the streets, at the dinner table, or against the brass at the local pub, all wanted the same thing: an enjoyable life. *Parts Unknown* stood as the last real bastion of counterculture America represented in the mainstream. Bourdain created cinema-inspired television on a network, a feat that changed the face of CNN from a talking head machine into a place of experience and stories. Anthony Bourdain let the squares inside his orgy of life.

While Bourdain hit the nicest of the nice, he also slummed. It wasn't about luxury or the number of Michelin stars dangling from a restaurant's name, it was about the experience. He had drinks made from spit and cow's blood. He devoured a fresh caught snapper on the beach, pulled from the cooler of a local who couldn't speak a lick of English. The narrative never changed: love the people, learn their secrets.

Bourdain and his Zero Point Zero crew made television that wasn't a bunch of fat white guys guffawing over a local beer and burger joint. Instead, they saw their chance to make high art, to challenge viewers and take them on the journey. The look and feel of his shows were never a hatchet job. The narration, the vibe—everything was pored over. Cultural notes like *Heart of Darkness*, the movies of Federico Fellini, and the car chases of Steve McQueen all permeated the landscape of the show. Bands like Queens of The Stone Age and The Black Keys wanted their songs featured. Margo Price, Ume, The Sword, and even the godfather of punk Iggy Pop all got to experience the world of Bourdain. His work pivoted around the love of art, no matter the medium. Every shot mattered. The writing on the show was brilliant, honest, and true. While Bourdain's books and essays are testaments to his writing prowess, it was the guttural rawness of his scripts that ached, begging the viewer to travel, eat, and experience life.

The honesty of the subjects he took on is what made me adore Anthony Bourdain. He took us to Montana, to

EXISTENTIAL THIRST TRAP

Madagascar, to Moscow. I saw the streets of my old stomping grounds in New Orleans alongside the tragedies of Iran and Myanmar. When Anthony Bourdain visited West Virginia, he handled the opioid crisis with care and humanity. He showed character: it wasn't devastation porn but a portrait of a neglected America.

He was a brilliant writer, a storied cook, a former addict—the guy I wanted to talk to at the party. And now he's gone.

Brian Allen Carr summed up Anthony Bourdain with an homage that was genuine, respectful, and stabs like a dagger: "Anthony Bourdain was Hunter Thompson, Fernand Point, and Studs Terkel wrapped up in one. He's the reason America eats at food trucks. He's the reason we take pictures of all our food. If you've Yelped, it's because of him. He was the most significant writer in recent memory."

Goddammit, Tony. I'm going to miss you.

THE ROTTEN HEART OF LOVE

BEING LONELY IN a home you share with someone stings harder than actually being alone. The feeling of my marriage dying was worse than any cliché constructed from the paper-mâché of countless divorce filings.

When my wife told me she wanted to call it quits, it felt like a cruel joke.

"You can't be serious," I think I said.

She was. I didn't believe her. We had two boys, a house, and a dog. But I knew. Over is over. Our number was up.

In retrospect, I knew she was right. The mix of complacency and misery was a cocktail neither of us was willing to swallow any longer. We didn't hate one another. There were no screaming matches. Doors weren't slammed and our kids were oblivious. It was just over. Two people once so passionately in love that their desire stretched across state lines were another broken home.

Before we'd officially wrapped our marriage up, I had to visit Chicago to bury one of my best friends. What a fucking dumpster fire. I drove to Lincoln Park Zoo alone. I didn't want any company. When I lived in Chicago, I'd walk the zoo to get clarity when times were tough. I needed that dependable salve of lions roaring and children lost in wonder staring at the penguins tapping on their ice. On my way, Tyler Childers's "Nose on the Grindstone" hit me like a ton of bricks. I burst into tears driving along the

EXISTENTIAL THIRST TRAP

Stevenson Expressway. Now, that place, time, sound, and feeling are all wrapped up together, and they'll stay that way forever.

For me, music is an emotional mile marker. I never forget where I was when I heard a particular song. I can explain how a record affects me on multiple levels. Music is a diary for the person I was and am, omnipresent. I remember the dead from the songs we shared. Amy Winehouse, Kurt Cobain, Layne Stanley—their music links me to them, to who I was, and to the people I loved when we were still dancing together, flailing hard in the pit. During the disintegration of my marriage, I retreated into the safe space of music, diving deeply into the recordings that touched me most. One of my favorites was *Alice in Chains*.

When Alice in Chains was approached about doing *MTV Unplugged*, it had been a long time since they'd last played together. Layne Staley was a full-blown junkie, lost in a sea of multi-platinum-strength heroin. The band had released their latest record a year prior in 1995 but never toured on it. Yet, on April 10th, 1996, the band emerged at the Brooklyn Academy of Music's Majestic Theatre. They took their seats on a dark stage lit with giant white candles and broken lava lamps, surrounded by the ghosts of the past. There's a saying about the *Alice in Chains* record, that "it's the sound of a man singing at his own funeral." They're not wrong. The collection of songs, "Over Now," "Angry Chair," and the masterpiece opening, "Nutshell," set the stage for a night that claws into my soul. It refuses to let go.

Alice in Chains was always this dark enigma. They were different, moody, more feral than their contemporaries. As a kid, I loved their depth, scrounging up change to buy a used copy of *Dirt*. By the time *Unplugged* aired, I was a fan. I planned to make a night of it. I got my VHS tape and recorded the show so I could watch it over and over again.

Unlike the emotional interpretation of Nirvana *Unplugged*, which feels like you're inside a funeral parlor, Alice in Chains's performance feels like purgatory.

The show is marked with an observation of the moment: our singer is fragile, broken, and rarely able to perform thanks to his problems, but we're here. It's a communion. It's sex with an ex who blew your mind but broke your heart. *Unplugged* is the second to last performance we ever got out of Staley. His final performance would be opening for Kiss after Stone Temple Pilots had to drop out. Staley overdosed after the show.

Unplugged is a chilling portrait of the tragic downfall of one of rock's most charismatic and enigmatic singers: a black-clad, pink-haired junkie slithers into his seat, his sunglasses hide his eyes awash with smack. His long sleeves cover the track marks on his arms. Still, he gives the performance of a lifetime, daring the cosmos, despite the poison. As Jerry Cantrell strums the opening chords of "Nutshell" while bassist Mike Inez slides down the neck of his bass and drummer Sean Kinney holds the beat, it's Staley who transfixes the moment, groaning,

> *We chase misprinted lies*
> *We face the path of time*
> *And yet I fight*
> *And yet I fight this battle all alone*
> *No one to cry to*
> *No place to call home*

His words seeped out from a primordial, fucked up internal swamp. That's master level bleak. You've had to sling a lot of emotional garbage to feel *that* alone. It put my own pain in perspective, for sure. Feeling so absolutely wasted stripped away my preconceived notion of what depression looked like. The album dared my demons to meet Layne's.

EXISTENTIAL THIRST TRAP

"Nutshell" exists in a universe of pain and sadness beyond regular emotional orbit. It's a standout from the *Jar of Flies* EP, but played *Unplugged*, it becomes its own entity. Staley's vocals come precisely on Kinney's beat. As Cantrell and Staley harmonize, they transport the listener in the moments they share. The duet defines two people's histories, linked by success and tragedy—something many of us feel on a microcosmic level. Listening, I feel like Alice in Chains might have felt then, the gris-gris of loss staining our bones.

Every thirteen seconds, someone in America gets divorced. Almost three hundred legal splits are approved every hour, equaling almost three million a year. That's a lot of families torn apart, for-sale signs, and golf clubs and vinyl records thrown on the lawn. With rates that rival divorce, millions of perfectly good humans are destroyed by addiction too. Lives are ruined by the magic in small baggies meant to take the pain away.

After I'd moved out of my house, I was dead inside. I moved into my best friend's place, downsizing from my family home to a single private room. All of my things, my books—my life, beyond the basics—sit in storage, waiting for me. Moving in, I felt defeated. There was no amount of Jameson or women to numb the pain. I was walking wounded.

So, what did I do? I poisoned myself, like Layne. I'm not a mean person, but thanks to anxiety, I can't forget my fuck-ups. As a result, I've watched most things slip through my grip like sand.

When Alice in Chains *Unplugged* dropped, a lot of the critics hated it. *Rolling Stone* and *Spin* both panned the performance, citing some hooey about "lack of electricity." In case they missed the memo, Layne Staley was *Weekend at Bernie's* propped up there on the stage. In the past, you'd see live Alice in Chains gigs, and Staley could be in a suit or shirtless. Back then, he was a guile mad man, hell-bent on rock and roll. In the *Unplugged* performance, a heroin-soaked half-grin replaced the once glowing maniacal smile. But despite the smack surging through him, Staley gave us his all. And it's not like Jerry Cantrell, Mike Inez, and Sean Kinney didn't show up for work. *Unplugged* is a flawless musical performance. The signature sludge is there, and the songs ring true. Acoustically, their bellicose, haunting vibe becomes a narration for the damned. "Over Now" doesn't feel steeped in finality, but acoustically, it almost seems hopeful, despite the lyrical content.

I aspired to that kind of balance, and I clutched at *Unplugged* as my life fell apart. Looking at the relationship I once held like a small, secret gem and realizing it no longer shone jabbed at my soul. Even when I was miserable and confused and hurt by how Sarah and I interacted with one another, I never lost my adoration for my wife. Only after our bonds were broken and I'd slept on the couch a few times did I realize it wasn't all about me. The split was about *everyone's* happiness. Moving on from that would fuck anyone up.

There was the emotional part of it, but I had to deal with the practical stuff too. For example, I couldn't figure out how to get my wedding band off. After six years of wearing it, I'd gotten fatter and the band was stuck. After some research, I went to Walgreens and got a pack of cinnamon dental floss. Sitting in Sarah's chair, I twisted the scented twine around my finger like a corkscrew. Within a few pulls, the ring came off, one turn at a time. And finally, I was holding this token that now was meaningless, the shedding of an axiom.

"We pay our debts sometimes." Yeah, we do, Layne.

My favorite thing about *Unplugged* is its atmosphere of emotional wisdom. There aren't the typical hoots and hollers. Rather, Staley does his best to respond to the room's aura. The band was rusty since it had been years

EXISTENTIAL THIRST TRAP

since playing together, but they soldiered on. They kept moving—just like I had to too.

Being single taught me humility, fast. I remembered what it was like to talk to new people with purpose. I might have that safe, married-guy game when I flirted around the office or gave a wink to the cute cashier at the gas station, but once I was dragging life's waters looking for someone to make out with, I could see my flaws in vivid technicolor. I had to leave my ghosts at the door, to the best of my ability. Trying, that's what was important. The art of being alone was a new feeling that's not unlike drugs. There were highs. The lows bite with a venom that reminded me that the world can be a landmine-filled hellscape. More than once, I caught a glimpse of shirtless single me and thought, *Bitch, you're* gross.

See my heart, I decorate it like a grave
You don't understand who they thought I was supposed
to be
Look at me now, a man who won't let himself be

In a 1996 interview with *Rolling Stone*—his first in a long time—Layne Staley tried his hardest to come off as normal. But he wasn't. The piece highlighted the band's triumphs with the self-titled record and the *Unplugged* performance. Staley addressed the fact that most people thought of him as a mindless junkie incapable of much. The assumptions that he was dead bothered him, leading him to say, "I'm gonna be here for a long fuckin' time."

He lasted six more years. I'm scared of death, especially death by my hand. I'm scared of where I would go. Committing to someone and making the lifetime pact that we're ride-or-die weighed on me. The thought of giving my heart to my partner was a formidable obstacle for me. Losing that commitment to Sarah felt like starting over emotionally. Like, if the flesh does not bind us, then what does it all mean?

Alice in Chains broke up for a brief time too. They didn't know what to do with a drummer lost in a bottle, an apathetic genius for a guitar player, and a singer stuck in a chasm of drugs. I get that. Divorce of any kind changes how you see yourself. It changes the context. Losing your emotional identity, that's a different ball of wax. Leaving a relationship or a band can be an act of self-preservation—something anyone who's been broken-hearted knows too well. Sometimes a band can ruin you, just as a partner can.

There's no bitterness between me and Sarah. We're better friends than we were spouses. We're probably best friends in some weird bizarro universe shit. We're a team dedicated to the success of two little humans we made together. These days, I have my boys on the weekend. I used to avoid their questions about why I live with Preston now and only drop them off at home. Now, we're all cool. They get it. We all get it. They get a lot of ice cream and cheeseburgers. We go to the batting cages. We shop for Halloween decorations because it's their favorite holiday. My failure with their mother doesn't define the love for my sons.

After their bedtime at the house we used to share, I roll down the windows and drive. There's never a destination. Austin at night is a sleepy place. It's different than Chicago or New Orleans. I explore the streets, letting the cool rain fall on my arm and dampen the inside of my car. Many nights, I'll have on Alice in Chains *Unplugged*. The city is asleep, but I'm wide awake, already working out tomorrow.

> *I don't mind, yeah*
> *Lost my mind, yeah*
> *Can't find it anywhere*

Divorce teaches a hard truth. I'm unplugged now. I'm a broken lamp sitting at Goodwill waiting for the right set of hands and a new place to sit. You've got the cracks, scars,

EXISTENTIAL THIRST TRAP

and chips, but some bohemian out there is into that shit. Alice In Chains got a new singer, he's great. My life will be great too.

When Layne Staley got up after the *Unplugged* performance, he looked elated, like the fire inside was still there, that maybe he could kick. He never did. Before his exit, he spoke into the mic saying, "I wish I could just hug you all, but I'm not gonna."

He walked offstage into an eternity of what could have been. We pay our debts sometimes indeed. With our hearts. Through love and death.

PART THREE:

GOOD MEN AND GATORS

PLEASE, DON'T PASS THE CAKE.

THERE'S AN ATROCITY taking place in homes across America, and we're gonna talk about it. Almost as critical as climate change, just a tier below bees dying off in droves, and somewhere in the shadow of the JFK assassination. This problem runs deeper than religions, creeds, and political affiliation. Whether you're a Muslim, Christian, or Jew, Democrat or Republican, Boomer or Millennial, it's time to address the elephant in the room.

Why is a group of misinformed savages acting like cake is equal to pie?

The fuck it is.

Created by the Egyptians, propagated by the Greeks, made substantial by the Germans, and driven home by post-industrial age Americans, cake has become the symbol of birthdays, weddings, and death. Someone gets married and wants to take a tacky photo with a slice? Cake has your back. Grandma kick the bucket? Here, have a slice of sympathy sponge.

Pie doesn't get caught up in all that nonsense. It's humble, more meaningful. You might eat cake when grandma dies, but you share her pie while she's alive.

And where's cake? You get one on your birthday, which is constructed to be a work of homespun art while everyone pretends to be happy that you wheezed all over it, blowing out the candle. Tally it all up: spit, waxy candle bits, layers of frosted drywall no one actually wants to eat. Sounds delicious!

Kids' birthday parties are even worse. We're stuffing an already insane batch of miscreants with hot dogs and chips, and then we give them a low-grade sugar surge? Who thought this was a good idea?

Let's get real here: have you even been to a birthday party where the whole cake is actually eaten? Sixty percent gets tossed about three days after guilt led you to stuff the leftovers in the beer fridge because "it'd be awful to let all that hard work go to waste." Truth is, we all know that festering pile of shit was just taking up critical real estate.

Hell with birthdays, what about our two biggest food holidays, Christmas and Thanksgiving? Any of y'all munching on cake? Nope. Your ass is lining up to sample nine different kinds of pie. You just stuffed yourself silly with mashed potatoes, turkey, and a food *that is called stuffing*, but you still managed to make room for pie. Why? Because it's that good.

How cake became viewed as pie's equal is a mystery of not only the Marvel universe but the real one we live in, and there ain't any friendly Spider dudes or cosmic dessert power like Thanos and his sparkly glove to redeem it.

Cake sucks. It's nothing more than a drywall center covered in disgusting icing with crunchy sugar cancer flowers—and without the frosting, cake is even worse. A loathsome sponge with no soul, reliant on blind hope all of the ingredients will coalesce. Let's get real, cake people, you're just in it for the frosting. And that's fine, I guess, but all the frosting in the world can't beat a simple peach pie.

A slice of pie has umami: the crunch of the crust, the gooey center. Let's stop patting cake on the head and giving it a participation trophy for just showing up. Cake is the kid on the tee ball team who loves sitting on the bench and slurping Slushies. He didn't earn his $5 star trophy with the sad little plaque, but he got it anyway, despite puking red at second base the one time he actually got a hit.

EXISTENTIAL THIRST TRAP

In the pantheon of dessert foods, cake is a 7th place, at best, behind cannoli, fritters, cobbler, and whatever fun things English people make on *The Great British Baking Show*.

Pie comes in apple, cherry, lemon meringue, pumpkin, strawberry, blueberry, and chess—it's such a rainbow of flavors, there should be a cartoon leprechaun guarding that shit. Who doesn't like a tangy key lime pie with its bright, bitter flavor, airy layer of whipped cream, and then your boy the graham cracker crust adding a flavor layer and coming correct Mack Diesel-style?

Over in Cakeville, the best you can hope for is red velvet, which is ultra-chocolate with red fuckin' dye. Every cake defender cites chocolate as the supreme example of cake's power, but have you tried chocolate pie? It's lush, velvety, with a pudding consistency, and, unlike chalky ole cake, doesn't require a glass of milk to cover for that drywall-tasting ass.

Cake has, like, six flavors: chocolate, red-chocolate, vanilla, vanilla with some colorful shit inside, and weird strawberry that tastes like the color pink. But Bobby, what about ice cream cake? Get out of here with that crap. That's ice cream in a fancy outfit. And as for cheesecake? The cream cheese texture and presence of a crust suggests it's more pie than cake. I'm chalking that up to marketing because "cheesecake" rolls off the tongue. "Cheese pie" sounds disgusting.

Cake can get stacked into crazy tiers or turned into a baby-eating witch, as TV competition shows have taught us. Cake came only to impress. It's the attractive asshole cousin who shits on every family get-together. Just because it looks fancy from afar doesn't mean it's beautiful. When it comes to getting to know cake, there's not much there.

A pie is art made out of a grandmother's embrace. You don't just make a crust, those little divots with a fork takes patience and someone willing to teach that skill. Pies are currency, acts of kindness when someone does something nice for you—ain't no one's name Duncan Hines.

Pie might as well shit eagles and fart fireworks. We don't say "as American as apple cake." Don McLean didn't drive his Chevy to the levy for some carrot cake. And all those horny teens didn't head to the movie theaters to laugh their asses off back in the early '00s when a teenaged everyman got caught with his dick in some angel food.

In cartoons, no one leaves a pound cake on the windowsill. Hell, Delmar, Delmar left a dollar for his thievery in *O Brother Where Art Thou*, back when a buck could feed a family for a year. Cake is a bourgeois representative of Ayn Rand-esque society of celebrating the self for sick pleasure, while the humble pie is a factotum of everyman deliciousness that working hands created out of nothing. Plus, there's a Robert E. Lee cake. If that isn't fucked up, what is?

THE SOUND OF
SKATEBOARD WHEELS

SOMETIMES, IT FEELS like staring into the sun is probably the easiest answer when trying to make sense of my life. Fuck it, we're doomed, why not burn out my corneas? Life is a weird-ass ride. People change, they grow apart, they start thinking Alex Jones is sane. It's a straight up circus out there, and we're all under the big top.

As I get older, life's only turned out more bizarre. I stopped trying to understand culture and instead simply observe it. Watch with intent. I have no idea who any of these popular motherfuckers are anyway. I'm no teenage girl. I don't want to get caught up either. I plan to keep reading books from people who've been taking the dirt nap since Eisenhower was in the Oval Office.

A few moments made me conscious of the mortal coil, but the big two were becoming a dad and my friend Matt's suicide. I never wanted to get married or have kids. I figured I'd roam the earth like Kane in *Kung Fu*. But now, I can't imagine my life without my two gremlins. Fatherhood is my north star, my bright spot. I know I've made a lot of mistakes and taken a lot of L's over the years, but little those dudes stand as my one unfuckwithable win. It balances out the darkness, most days. With the love, there comes a lot of loss.

This is how I found out Matt killed himself. I was

scrolling through Facebook and kept seeing people from my old neighborhood posting things like "I can't believe you're gone" and "I wish we could have known." Bad shit. You know what that means. A surge shot through me as I traced the links and saw my childhood best friend's name popping up over and over. I called his phone. I called his mother. When she had a moment, she called me back to tell me about Matt.

We talked, I listened, and I didn't cry. I didn't process it at that moment. It was like hearing dialogue from a movie. I told her I'd be at the funeral and promised to "write him something nice." What the fuck else could I say.

Matt was my best friend when I was 12, and we'd been tight since we were four years old. The sound of our friendship is skateboard wheels hitting concrete, 1990s punk, janky mixtapes, and the hustle of scrounging up a couple of bucks for a chili dog. For 34 years, our White Sox hats signaled a deeper love than being fans of a ball club. I can't remember life without Matt. He's embedded in my memories. He's woven into the fabric of my being.

When we discovered skateboarding, we begged our parents to buy us flea market, garage sale, second-hand skateboards—cheap, didn't matter. We'd ride anything with four wheels and the ability to ollie. We took scrap from dumpsters, new houses. We stole anything that wasn't locked down and built the worst child-mangling ramps we could put together (don't judge, it was a different time). Matt and I sucked. But we were obsessed anyway, trying to land the big tricks and failing every time.

Once, we were in downtown Chicago near a hotel where the bottles all faced out in a giant, glittering wall of glass. It was beautiful. We were trying to kickflip over the curbs when legendary sportscaster Harry Caray stumbled out, drunk as a skunk. We yelled his name. Being a man of the people, Harry gave us a one-armed salute with a roaring, intoxicated *hey hey* just before he fell into his cab.

EXISTENTIAL THIRST TRAP

We hated the Cubs. But we thought it was the coolest thing ever. We'd never seen a "famous" person before.

Above all, we loved the White Sox. By the time we were ten years old, we were trading with every kid in the neighborhood for White Sox cards, always ditching Cubs players before they poisoned our collections. We went to a lot of games. We saw Ventura, Thomas, and Ozzie. And when the White Sox won in 2005, we called one another. Our team finally did it.

Me and Matt and my Grammie were a trio, back in the day. Matt was family. The women in my family called him "red-headed Matt." Grammie took us everywhere. Someone hooked her up with the cheater box—a dude in the hood would climb a pole and give you cable for $50. Most weekends, Matt and I would sit up all night watching R-rated movies while everyone else was asleep.

In high school, we used to do one another's homework. We were yin and yang with school. I crushed English and sucked at math. Couldn't do the essential times tables. Matt was the exact opposite. The man couldn't spell "the bird is in the cage," but he could figure out your taxes on a dinner napkin like he was tying shoes. Once, he did my math homework for me. I got an A+, and my teacher was so excited. She thought I'd had a breakthrough in pre-algebra (I was a senior. It was so sad.). In exchange for that A+, I'd written Matt a paper. Only *his* teacher asked him to stay after class. He knew immediately Matt didn't write it and made him do it over. After that, I learned to make mistakes on purpose.

After we got our driver's licenses, Matt scored a broken-down minivan, and my God, did we think it was the coolest thing ever. Other kids had these crappy little cars. Matt had a *van*. We could fit so many people in that thing. We'd cruise around the South Side, blasting Misfits tapes and acting cool—Matt behind the wheel, me riding shotgun.

A few years later, we discovered *Jackass*. Whatever they did, we groaned, "We coulda got paid to do that!" And, just like all the other dudes who saw the show, we eventually accepted the fact that we could probably take a swift kick to the junk but not handle doing a swan dive from the roof onto a glass table. We tried the smaller stuff instead. One day, we were hanging around at my friend Eddy's mom's place. Matt and I had heard about "the milk challenge," predicated on the idea that the human stomach can't handle a gallon of milk. Chugging that much was a guarantee you'd puke—a lot.

It was a summer night. Us two jerks were spewing hot milk puke all over Eddy's mom's flowers. And her garden. And the grass. She came out screaming. We laughed so hard that we had tears in our eyes while this poor woman was freaking out. We ended up having to clean it all up with Palmolive and a garden hose. I took those silly moments for granted. There's so much left unsaid, so much time wasted. I have my sweeter reminiscences too, but the fact is that Matt was fun. We were good together. We got up to shit I couldn't imagine doing with anyone else. No matter what I was into, what stupid thing I was working on, Matt was there for it. He never wavered. He was my rock, always there. He told me how proud he was when I released a book. When an article went live, he'd share it, say to his friends that he had a friend who was a writer.

That touched me. I wish I'd seen him more. I owe a lot to him for being my friend, and it didn't dawn on me till I read a lot of these memories as I gave his eulogy at his funeral. Those small moments of truth wrapped in love.

Over the years, we grew apart as life happened. I moved to New Orleans and then to Austin. Matt became a millwright and moved to Indiana. But we never lost touch. The thing is, I don't know if I ever told Matt how much respect I had for the life he chose. I think I'll always regret that. Thing is, we're from the South Side. Our people work

EXISTENTIAL THIRST TRAP

with their hands, and Matt followed in that tradition. Tradesmen like Matt built Chicago by doing the jobs that mean something for the infrastructure of our world. We never let distance or time affect our friendship. We texted, and any time we saw one another, it was like we'd never been apart. We never lost a page in the book, even if it had fewer entries lately.

After his son died unexpectedly, Nick Cave described grieving as feeling like "tiny, trembling clusters of atoms subsumed within grief's awesome presence. It occupies the core of our being and extends through our fingers to the limits of the universe. Within that whirling gyre, all manner of madnesses exist; ghosts and spirits and dream visitations, and everything else that we, in our anguish, will into existence. These are precious gifts that are as valid and as real as we need them to be. They are the spirit guides that lead us out of the darkness."

That was how I felt about Matt. When I love, I know that the other side of that coin is grief. When I give my heart over to someone, it's part of the unspoken deal that while I have you right now, later on, I will mourn you with an ache that stings. Grief is a hideous reminder of how small I am compared to the vastness of what life holds in store.

When I got to the funeral, people I hadn't seen in decades were surprised to see me. They acted like I was a ghost who'd blown in to bury another specter. I gave Matt's eulogy, and I'm glad someone could speak up for him because the priest didn't know what the fuck he was saying. That was just words, throwaway lines from his notes. I've given a lot of final words over the years, but this time, I gave it my heart. It was the least I could do. I felt the weight of Matt's body when I carried him home on my shoulders with the others.

After the service, we racked up hefty tabs down at the tavern. I drank till five in the morning, and my brothers and I talked shit till the sun peeked through the clouds. We did it because it was mandatory. That's how we do memorials: swapping stories, talking about life, and wondering about where the road would take us.

I think about Matt often as things change in my life, as doors open and close. When he took his own life, I had a ton of questions. Why did he leave us? Couldn't we have talked it out? What about his family? What about our friendship? None of that matters now. It's been a while and I'm still thinking about it. All I can do now is remember when it was awesome. I don't dwell on his absence. I remember the redhead at the end of the ramp and how eager we were for our skateboards, looking out at a world of possibility.

OLD DUDES

"LEMME KNOW WHEN you'll be back in town so I can prepare to ruin my life for a few days." That's how I say goodbye to my pals. The last time I said it, I was leaving my usual haunt of Galveston, a tiny beach island just south of Houston. My painter buddy Derek hugged me goodbye. I love Galveston because it's ancient and has resisted the gentrification that scarfs down every other decent place on the face of the earth. There are no high-end sneaker shops or tourist traps. Instead, it's got cheap shrimp pulled right out of the gulf's waters, a low-key beach, and these beautiful old houses built during the turn of the century. Derek and I spent a week running those quiet streets, and it was the best therapy I know.

Another reason I love it is you can still smoke in the bars. I don't know if that's legal or not, but I'm not complaining. Everything on the island smells like seventeen layers of Pall Mall smoke. Galveston is a lawless wonderland for drinkers who love a good jukebox and conversation. Suits me just dandy.

Galveston keeps me coming back with a thriving dive bar culture. Insane locals cruise around on jacked-up golf carts with sound systems blaring country music. I met men who live like pirates, random weirdo artists, women with non-ironic hand tattoos, and a whole smorgasbord of drunks living out their lives one well tequila at a time. There is also a solid stock of old island freaks. Give me Charlie, the retired construction worker who hates everyone. Or the woman who will passionately explain string theory even though she's been hitting the Stoli since *Wheel of Fortune* came on four hours ago. One evening, Derek and I ended up in The Albatross, an extra crispy dive off the Strand. We met this cat, a former Navy SEAL who'd set every record for skydiving. He told us stories about tours of duty, jump school, and working on missions in places where everyone most definitely wanted him dead. He showed me his wall of fame, photos of him ripping through the sky. The guy was in his mid-70s and spry, smart, and willing to spill his guts about his life. We should all be so lucky to soak up the history of life from older folks. I didn't get to hear any deep insights on government-sanctioned murders, but he did leave a fish dangling on the hook: "Maybe next time you're in town, since we're buddies now."

No matter where I am globally, my usual M.O. is to ask someone what the worst bar in town is, and I go straight there. Show me a musty, rusted-out room that hasn't been dusted since the Nixon administration and I'm down. There's something magical about those places. Out of the blue, you'll hear war stories: lost loves, deaths, friendships that danced on the edge of sanity, the good times and the bad ones.

Back in New Orleans, there's a bar off Tchoupitoulas Street—45 Tchoup—where I was stopping regularly. One day, I rolled in with a few books under my arm and posted up (it's perfectly acceptable in New Orleans to grab a seat and read). Dives in New Orleans can't shake the scent of cigars and cigarettes etched into the oak. The light only peeks through the glass. It never allows the lamination to affect the mood. That's perfect for reading. It's like a library, but with Jack Daniels.

I was reading when an old-timer finished his copy of the day's *Times-Picayune* and had recognized the book I was reading, James Ellroy's *American Tabloid*. It goes deep on the mob, Kennedy, life in the 60s, and is hyperviolent. The old cat motioned me to come down to the corner seat. His voice was a creaky, deep New Orleanian sandpaper accent. He'd seen action over the years. The fellow didn't order—he gave the nod.

We talked about books, the South Side of Chicago. I mentioned that my great grandfather, Miner, was a bootlegger for Capone. Immediately, the gray-hair's ears perked up. After a few drinks, he leaned in, offering New Orleans trade secrets.

"The fuckin' Quarta, all them buildings? Mob owned. We bought all that shit back in the day. Now, all the people rent 'em from us. Probably four families own Bourbon and Royal Street. Might be a name on the lease or scribble on the deed, but that's old money, son."

Leaning in and pointing to my book, he poked a timeworn finger at the cover. "See this Kennedy? Homegrown. Carlos Marcello. We did that shit. Fuckin' Joe Kennedy was cleaning the money for our people. We made him three times his cash. We put his kid in the White House. What's the fuckin' kid do? He starts talkin' all this racial shit. We're old school Italians. He's talkin' this man-on-the-moon shit. And he goes and puts that punk motherfucker Bobby Kennedy as his Attorney General! First fuckin' thing that guy does is go after us! We put his brother in office, and now this motherfucker comes after us after the Bay of Pigs thing? The fuck outta here."

He took a rip off his scotch. This dude could mollywop me, even at his advanced age. He hit a lick again. "Oswald was a fuckin' stooge. Some patsy. Jack Ruby? Look at that man's history. He was mobbed up but owed debts. Jack Ruby was a two-bit hustlin' fuck. Ruby didn't have no juice. He was a nightclub owner who was in deep to Marcello. It was die by us or go out a legend. The Warren Commission says one thing, but, kid, that's smoke and mirrors. He was in over his head and he knew it. Ruby wasn't no patriot."

ROBERT DEAN

I listened all day. I never saw that old-timer again.

One summer, I was back home visiting Chicago. My parents live in a suburb called Lockport, just outside the city. It's your typical South Side working class outpost, full of white flight trades workers who are openly homophobic and racist. But whatever, this ain't about those creeps. My brothers, Brandon and Bryan, and I needed haircuts. They knew of a spot over off State Street that I'd long forgotten. Back in the day, there were two barber shops in town, coincidentally a few doors down from one another. This is a big no-no in barber culture. I know this because I learned all about what's kosher with guys who cut hair on this day.

If you're not hip, barbershops go one of three ways: neighborhood hangout where guys flock to talk shit; the retro "cool" shop where each barber has an ironic mustache and wears a smock and listens to nothing but classic rockabilly; and then there's the old school joint where the owner couldn't give a fuck less about being cool, he wants to make his daily bread and go home. This spot fell into the third category. It was in business when my parents moved to Lockport back in 1996 and evident that this barber had run the shop generations before by his slacks and short sleeve button up.

In true Lockport fashion, the place stunk like old cigarette smoke, thanks to the wooden paneling that hadn't been updated since the turn of the century. The signs that hung on the walls evoked the Ford administration, complete with faded White Sox pennants. The ubiquitous busty girl calendar was stuck in January 1987. The old cat saw the three of us walking in and gave us the "hold up" finger so he could finish eating his Chinese food, which added some extra funky-ass depth to the smell of the room. After he'd finished chowing down on his egg roll, he lit a smoke; and as it dangled off his bottom lip, he motioned to his chair.

"Which one of you assholes is first?"

EXISTENTIAL THIRST TRAP

At first, my haircut was a relatively average experience. He asked about all of my tattoos. He talked about the Sox and their usual woes, dropping a well-placed "cocksucker" or "motherfucker" in every interaction between one of the three of us. When one cigarette would burn out, a new one took its place at once. On his workbench—next to the clippers, shears, pomades, and oils—was a bottle of Windex. Cutting my brother Bryan's hair, he finished up with a tight neckline, and instead of using the traditional talc or aftershave, he grabs the Windex and sprays it on my brother.

"Did you just use Windex on my neck?"

"What? It's the same shit, ain't it? Fuckin' alcohol, kid. Smells good too."

Now, the barber did give a solid haircut. When it was my turn to sit in the chair, one of us made a casual mention about the shop a few doors down, asked if they might be friends.

"I hate that motherfucker with every bone in my body!" I thought he was going to lop my goddamn ear off the way he carried on. "I've been here since the fucking seventies, and this piece of shit opens up sometime around when you were babies. There's a barber's code! You never open up a shop next to another man. This is my area. You got a whole fucking town to service! I established the business. What if I'm busy and someone walks down? Instead of waiting, they'll go sit in his fucking shop if the wait is shorter! That piece of fucking dog shit. He broke the code of the barber! We used to throw bricks through one another's windows. I tried to light his building on fire. I'd leave him notes telling him what a piece of shit he was. He'd go to the gun range and leave me the paper with all the holes in it. Fucking scumbag."

It didn't matter what our opinions were because he kept going. I was *living*.

"That rat bastard dropped from a heart attack not too

long ago. Best day of my life. I'm here cutting hair, and all of the ambulances pull up with their lights and sirens, I see them pulling him out on the little cart."

"The gurney?" I asked.

"Yeah, whatever. They had the mask on him and everything, and I ran right up to the bastard and gave him a big *ha-ha, you piece of shit! I'll see you in hell!* And I spit on the front door of his place as they drove off. Not too long later, he died. I had a few Miller Lites to celebrate the occasion."

That haircut was well over a decade ago, and the Windex-spritzing barber is dead too. Two new places operate in those spaces. I'm sure they don't hate one another with the same passion, which I think is kind of a shame. What sticks with me is: what happened when it was over—when his rival was dead and gone? Was the battle better than the eventual victory? Did he find something to love about hating someone so much, for so many years? As a future old man, I make a study of these strangers. That'll be me one day, if I get lucky. And when I roll up to my last days, I fully intend to be ready.

DINOSAUR SKULLS

WHAT'S MY FATHER LIKE? Well, when he was 15, he and my uncle beat up the ice cream man, stole the ice cream truck, and drove around Canaryville handing out ice cream cones. It was a good day on the South Side. These days, Bob clocks in around 5'10" and 220 pounds. He wears black everything and rocks a gray beard with a salt and pepper mane. He is the textbook biker dude.

He is funny, interesting, and weird. He's got his GED but can tell you about the Giza pyramids, the internal combustion engine, and the basics of thermodynamics. He's been loading trucks at the same spot my whole life, but if you ask him how to rewire your kitchen, he can draw it on a bar napkin. He cuts up with strangers, can explain the fine nuance of hanging drywall correctly, and tells real-life stories straight from the John Dillinger files.

I'm getting old. It's weird. Every day, there's a new patch of gray invading my beard. Those grays make me mortal; they force me to accept my age. What the hell happened? The clock is a cruel mistress; it never stops. My parents aren't the same rock and roll, Harley-riding gangsters anymore. *My* kids are getting older; they call me "Dude." It fucks with my head. When I look in the mirror, I see my old man. I used to look like my mom, now I look like my dad.

My mother, Janet, is the steady hand in my parents'

relationship. She's blonde, honest, and direct. Despite not living in the same state as them since I was 27, talking to my parents is a joy. During the coronavirus horror show, I doubly appreciated them. The folks who raised me are a fucking gift.

A decade-plus ago, when I told my parents I was leaving Chicago for New Orleans, they thought I wasn't serious. I remember my dad exclaiming, "Why would you wanna live down there? All they do is shoot one another." (Somehow, Chicago was the picture of civic unity.)

Once I settled in, though, I invited them down. Come see how the other half lives. My father converted easily. Within the first hour of his first trip, he was guzzling free Miller Lites thanks to my friends on Bourbon Street. Gratis shots of Jack Daniels have a way of making even the harshest critics come around.

"Okay, this ain't so bad," he said. "I'm gonna be shitfaced before lunch."

I reminded him that it's Bourbon Street's job.

"Better get me a diaper, then."

Bob's got quirks. For example, do not play with his food. If you want to die a slow, painful death of rapid complaints, order him a ribeye.

He turns up his nose, saying, "I ain't eating this! Look at all the fat on this meat!"

Don't even ask about sushi.

One time, I went up to Chicago to visit with my kids and my then-wife. I was outside on the phone when my ex walked over to let me know that my dad was mad about the pizza. (For the record, Chicago pizza is thin crust, tavern cut squares. We consider deep dish to be a satanic tool of food media.) True to his roots, my dad absolutely *hated* deep dish.

"Been married for almost forty years, and when have you ever seen me order a deep dish? I like regular pizza, not this bullshit!" he was carrying on. My mom played

EXISTENTIAL THIRST TRAP

devil's advocate, hoping he'd eat it, which did not execute well. Bob was mad about pizza. I can't say I blame him.

With that said, Bob's a good guy. You can stick him in any room and he'll make friends. Throw him out of a plane over Peru, and within an hour, he'll find out where to fish, and twenty minutes later, some old man with a hand-made pole is sharing hooch. You could say I take after him, and that would be a compliment. There are a few places where we differ, though, and that's where things get funny.

For example, my dad cannot stand anything that smells bad. He's got the olfactory senses of an African elephant. It's a guarantee that he'll lose his shit. One winter, my brothers and I were in his Chevy Blazer, coming home from our Grammie's place in Canaryville. It was the kind of weather where your spit freezes before it hits the snow. I was thirteen at the time; my twin brothers were eight. One of them laid a brutal fart.

In an instant, the old man started gagging. He opened his window even though the snow was coming in. He yelled, "Come on, man! Quit blowing farts in the car!"

The rest of us were trying to keep it together. His fuse was lit, and it was *hilarious*. Once Bob got going, forget it. A few more miles toward our place, and my brother dropped another devastator.

"Come on, man! Why didn't you shit before we left?"

From the passenger seat, my mom was trying to speak with authority through her laughter, but a complete sentence was too much. Bob pulled off Archer Avenue and into an alley somewhere near Pulaski. He got out and yanked open my brother's door.

"Do you need to take a shit?" he shouted. Snowflakes fell on his head and steam rose from his body. He was a monster, hell-bent on making my brother drop anchor in an alley next to some garbage cans. I laughed so hard I nearly shit myself.

I would like to say he mellowed with age, but Bob

retained his quirks. Over the years, my parents came to New Orleans a lot. As the trips progressed, they cared less about touristy stuff, but they were always themselves. Half of our time was spent getting drunk at my friends' bars. During one trip, we'd wrapped up eating shrimp po' boys at Domilise's. We see a sign for a shop called "The Wooly Mammoth," which had skulls and taxidermy in the windows,

"I bet they've got cool stuff," my dad says in his Chicago accent. That got my attention. It's rare for Bob to make a request.

Getting out of the car, he announced, "I ate too much. I hope I don't blow a fart."

Notice how it's okay if *he* does it, but God forbid *you* blow one around him.

My mother sighed. After four decades, she's used to it.

Uptown New Orleans in the spring is stunning. This is that "Old South" that poets jerk off about. The jasmine and all of the pungent flowers spread their aromas through the air like lavish tendrils. We left that all behind and walked into The Wooly Mammoth and let the door swing closed behind us.

As we expected, the shop was pleasantly bizarre. It wasn't as creepy as your weird neighbor's basement, but there was plenty to gawk at. Mounted on every surface were death's head moths in shadow boxes, chimpanzee skeletons, and samples from every part of the animal kingdom, from alligator heads to squirrels in top hats.

My poor mother. What she's had to endure over the years. Bob dragged her to the Harley dealer and Bass Pro Shop. She was forced to listen to interminable stories about fishing and what's happening in the world of aquatic sports. Her only revenge seemed like a fair trade—making the old man hang out in the purgatory seating every department store has, where husbands converge in a silent semicircle hell. This little sideshow trip to the bone store

EXISTENTIAL THIRST TRAP

was going to cost Bob at least an hour of wait time at Macy's.

However, that was later—the Mammoth was *now*. My dad walked over to a stand with rotating baskets full of crystals and common fossils. He pulled a small fossil out, an ammonite, and stared at it.

He said, "See this thing? It was crawling around, living, and it died. Now *millions* of years later, we're in this store. I'm holding it. I can *buy* it."

Did I mention that my dad smokes a ton of ultra-kush old man weed?

Walking around the shop, he kept the ammonite in his grip. He looked around, mumbling how cool everything was. My mom loitered by the register, already over this entire experience in morbidity. I had my eye on a gorilla skull, which was straight out of *National Geographic*.

Bob held on to his fossil, his portal to the past. He stopped at the counter where the sales associate was standing. He made small talk, but then he lowered his eyes to the case. Game over. It was filled with dinosaur bones. Dinosaurs are his *shit*.

"I was watching this special. There are a few scientists who don't think the meteor wiped them out," he said. The old man was into documentaries and had seen every basic cable long-form piece, from Jesse James to *MythBusters*. He loved breaking down the delicate nuances of the JFK assassination and had a soft spot for government conspiracy theories.

He said, "What if it wasn't as bad as they thought it was? That most dinosaurs survived? They think it was something else."

I could tell he was excited to dispel his theory, but he paused for dramatic effect.

"They think they died from shit."

The woman behind the counter practically clutched her imaginary pearls. This was Bob's moment to shine.

"Dinosaurs are huge! Dropping big turds everywhere! There's a ton of them. There are big piles of shit. They're walking in it, screwing in it. Shit-covered eggs. Babies are popping out, taking their first steps in shit piles. That'd make anything sick. Scientists think all the piles of shit gave the dinosaurs diseases. If a T. Rex kills a Stegosaurus and it's munching on guts covered in crap, it's gonna puke. Think about their immune systems!"

This poor lady. She was just trying to make a sale.

"Well, uh, that's one theory," she said.

My mom and I were dying. Bob turned to us, shrugging. "What's so funny? It ain't like dinosaurs had bathrooms!"

Sensing that he'd failed to convince us, he bought the ammonite.

He loved that fossil. Still loves it. He shows it to me every time I visit. He keeps it in his toolbox. Feed him a few shots of whiskey and he'll show *anyone* who visits. Each time, he reminds them: This thing was once alive. Millions of years ago, it crawled the same earth we're camping on. It lived, it died, and now it's in your hand. What are the odds? Bob wants to know. In another million years, maybe they'll say the same about us.

I SAW THE LIGHT

HANK WILLIAMS HAS been my favorite singer since I was 20 and his music smashed me like a freewheeling haymaker. I remember the first time I heard his voice. I hit the brakes in the middle of the road, gasping at the intensity of "So Lonesome I Could Cry," during an NPR story, of all things. It's still my favorite song today.

It's my natural disposition to lean toward sadness (this may be the understatement of the century). Sitting in a dive, listening to sad country songs is medicine my soul needs. There's a difference between lonely and lonesome. I ain't hardly ever lonely. There ain't ever enough sunshine when you prefer the dark.

Hank's voice is the sound of gloom. It lives in my blood. He's sex, death, and religion, all wrapped up in a whiskey-soaked bandana and tied across your mouth, hostage style. Everything wrong and right with the suffering of life is imprinted in his music. Hank lived hard and died in the back of his Caddy on New Year's Day, 1953. He wasn't even thirty. His music peers into the unknown, a toe in the void. He was a flawed hero, and he left a trail of flame (Waylon chased Hank, just like the rest of us who study the Drifting Cowboy). His face is tattooed on my left wrist. He's always with me. Forever.

He's been a guiding light through all my bullshit. He stuck with me through the ups and downs of hard living, from girlfriends to an ex-wife. Now, I'm all for love. I think it's incredible. I'm just on the other side of it. Getting divorced is hard. Packing your stuff into boxes and trash bags is heartbreaking. Talking to your kids about moving out isn't awesome. Forget trying to find the new normal in any immediate time frame. After taking that Louisville Slugger to the chest, I started thinking critically about *who* fucked up. Every time, Hank was there for me.

Some relationships last for seven years, while ones with a lot of meaning can last seven months. The mile marker of time seems insignificant when the experience itself should bear the weight of value. My divorce is not the first time—and probably won't be the last—I've felt the sting of losing someone.

A long while back, living in New Orleans, I'd had an ugly breakup. It was all over but the shouting. Watching that relationship die in real-time was hard, but it was necessary. When it ended, I was alone in an empty house in the Treme neighborhood. I had a schedule that allowed for a little play since I worked Thursday through the weekend and worked a double on Mondays. A friend teased the idea of hitting Atlanta for a quick 48 hours. She said I should drive in to see her and cruise through one of my favorite bars in the world—the Clermont Lounge, a.k.a. the home of Absolute Sin. They serve shots in hospital-grade medicine cups alongside cheap tallboys. Ancient strippers grind behind the bar, and every weirdo in town is getting fucked up right alongside you. The Clermont Lounge is an acre of heaven with just enough hell sprinkled in for spice. Getting out of Dodge sounded perfect. I had no plans other than to drink as much as possible.

Within a few texts, I prepped my stuff to leave Monday night straight after my double. Luckily, it was the slow season, so I knew we'd be closed by midnight (the boss had the same schedule and did not want to keep the bar open longer than he had to). By 11:30, I was walking out of the

EXISTENTIAL THIRST TRAP

door and headed for my car, clutching a few cans of Red Bull. Clocking the miles toward Atlanta, I entered Alabama. The home of Hank. I was blasting his music on my iPod, headed straight for his grave via the proverbial "Lost Highway."

Somewhere around 4 a.m., out of my skull on energy drinks, I made it to the Oakwood Cemetery Annex. His grave is polished white marble with a guitar and a hat, a memorial to the man who changed country music. It is open 24/7. It was just me and his ghost. I'd brought a small bottle of Jameson. I got out of my silver Ford Mustang, sat on the AstroTurf, and drank in the stillness of the graveyard. The hum of my motor accompanied Hank's songs, which still played inside my car. No one came or called, I was alone with the bones of my hero.

Bleary-eyed, I finally pulled into Atlanta. I got what was advertised: long nights, brutal hangovers, and lipstick on my teeth. I am pretty sure I used a money gun in the strip club. I ate a sloppy burger at the Vortex, stopped by Holy Mother tattoo, and wound up wandering around the zoo because I wanted to see the pandas on my last morning in town. I exorcised my demons, showed them a good time.

Leaving town, I wasn't done with Hank. As the miles passed, I blared "Angel of Death" and "Lovesick Blues" and plenty of songs by Luke the Drifter, Hank's alter ego. His voice made my pain feel relatable, like we were in a club of miserable bastards together. That's why his legend endures. At one point or another, we're all miserable.

I stopped in Georgiana, an eye blink of a town. It was Hank's childhood home, a place where he lived before moving to Montgomery. They'd turned his boyhood house into a mini-museum, complete with an old woman who knew him. The house was nice enough, white and green with a long wraparound porch. There was a "fan club" house and a train car with Hank's name on it.

Walking up the faded concrete steps of 127 Rose Street,

I entered his space, which was probably meaningless to him once he had that Nashville cash in his pocket but meant the world to me. The walls were filled with folk art, photos, and tributes in every medium to the man who's been dead longer than he was ever alive. One of his guitars was in there too. This museum wasn't a high dollar operation but a labor of love. It was evident that to the people running it, his memory was essential for the culture. I took in the air of the town. There were no parades or tight security. The locals were probably wondering why so many people cared about some dead guy in a funny suit with music notes on the sleeves. I left with a sticker that declared I'M A HANK WILLIAMS FAN and an original program from his funeral—something I cherish to this day.

Headed back south to Montgomery, I stood at the foot of his statue. Hank was hunched over in that familiar pose that's been on every record cover since the ole boy met his maker. I looked through the glass of his official museum. I hated myself for getting there an hour too late. It was closed. Seeing inside, I saw more art, more photos, some guitars, and suits. They even had the car he took for his last ride. Had I not spent time looking at the pandas, I could have made it—but sometimes, life is for the living. I made peace with my choice and got back in my car, speeding off toward New Orleans.

Later on, I wrote the liner notes for a tribute record officially sanctioned by Hank's estate and the museum. That was a career highlight for me. I have an official tie to Hank Williams, even if it's as insignificant as a few words in a CD. But that victory is mine. I still swell with pride thinking about it. I have "So Lonesome I Could Cry" on 45 in my 1954 Rockola jukebox. It belonged to my grandparents; now, when the needle drops on that song, not only do I get to honor their memory by loving that machine, I also get to hear Hank in his purest form.

All these years later, I still yearn for the howls of a

EXISTENTIAL THIRST TRAP

broken man leading me toward the light. I've acquired a few scars along the way. My heart has been glued back together more than once. I keep going. Breakups changed me. Divorce changed me. Feeling down is part of the process. It hurts to feel unloved, but it's the experience of being alive. I've made it longer than Hank did. Love isn't one-size-fits-all.

I often think that when I dropped everything and hit the road, cars around me headed toward whatever fate. I pulled up to that graveyard thinking about the state of my affairs, but I did it with someone I'd given my soul to time and time again. He didn't have to say anything at all. I knew he was there. I didn't feel lonesome. His ethereal presence was enough.

WHAT ELSE SHOULD I SAY?

ONE OF THE hardest things to quantify for me still is the loss of Kurt Cobain. At 35, I think about his music, his legacy, constantly. No single band has done more for me as a person or emotionally as Nirvana. Nirvana has been my favorite band since I was around 11 or 12. I can't remember a life that's pre-Nirvana. While I liked other bands and enjoyed all of the other stuff happening in metal, punk, and grunge, Nirvana's chord struck the loudest. While I've had my ebbs and flows of how much I listen to their music, there's never an argument about their impact on my life. Kurt Cobain's 50th birthday was a springboard for a wealth of emotions that got me thinking about what was lost that spring of 1994.

Nirvana was proud to be outsiders. They did their own thing without remorse while wearing a coat of many colors. Nirvana's music was inclusive for everyone who wanted to be a part of the party—whether that sat well with Kurt or not. That was the allure of their music, their presence. They might not have been the best, or the most talented, or whatever, their appeal was how they made me feel in a world full of glossy bands like Poison or Guns N Roses. They took punk idealism and made it mainstream. They took what so many bands felt, said, and worked toward waving the flag of and blasted it out to our whole generation. Through Nirvana's social message of

EXISTENTIAL THIRST TRAP

Incesticide's liner notes, seeds were planted. They wrote, "At this point, I have a request for our fans. If any of you in any way hate homosexuals, people of different color, or women, please do this one favor for us—leave us the fuck alone! Don't come to our shows and don't buy our records."

When I was a kid, I re-read and obsessed about every lyric, every quote. Nirvana helped me see the world wasn't restricted to my white neighborhood full of working class Irish tough guys. I was one of the many people who found a lifeline in Nirvana. I needed to know about subcultures, genres outside the mainstream. Nirvana broke that door wide open. Their songs weren't some garbage about fucking chicks. I was getting the message about what it felt like to be an outsider. I think that's why their music still endures—because of its honesty.

While some pigeonhole Kurt as nothing more than an over-hyped junkie, I saw him as a figurehead that mirrored my problems. They were my favorite band at the time of his death, but what resonated more was my sense of another personal loss around the same time. When Kurt Cobain committed suicide, my grandmother had passed away from cancer at 54 a month earlier. When she passed, I lost one of the most important people in my life, arguably just as important as either of my parents. Now, my hero was dead too. I compounded both losses into one mutated ache. Nirvana's music became more to me than enjoying angst. It became about loss and recovery. With the tired cliché of "your music got me through so much" as a footnote to life, it's true for me. I leaned on the death of Kurt Cobain as another way to process the loss of someone I loved so much. When I sang Nirvana's songs, they weren't anthems of jaded youth to me. I was trying to process a world I wasn't close to understanding; and in a lot of ways, I still don't.

All of this music hit me like a sledgehammer. It was good to be a kid in the 90s. I got all of the rock and roll I could take, in all of its forms. Punk made me socially aware, Rage Against The Machine paved the way for my passion for politics. But Nirvana's music was raw, it was powerful and never suffered from a slump. A lot of bands release crappy albums, but not Nirvana. Like the Beatles, the loss of Kurt encapsulated the passing of a genre—it's one vision, forever. We'll always be left asking what and why, and what could've been.

Looking back on Kurt Cobain's legacy, I have so much to consider. So many feelings to sift through. It's still so hard to fathom, to consider, or to place my finger on why it felt like a dagger in the heart. Rock stars are meant to feel bigger than life, but Kurt felt like he was as big as my living room. It was his aloof attitude toward fame. Despite being millionaires with oodles of power, the band didn't follow up *Nevermind* with a slick collection of hits; instead, it was *In Utero*, which DGC thought would ruin them. It didn't. It only made them more endearing to what they were versus what they were perceived to be. Who else would take a platform as big as theirs—as the biggest band in the world—and write songs like "Rape Me" or "Frances Farmer Will Have Her Revenge on Seattle?" Who else would "squander" their precious *Unplugged* taping and fill it with obscure cover songs, only for it to become a heart-wrenching classic which defined the medium as a whole? That was their power and vision.

The world has changed considerably since Nirvana. But I still adore their legacy, and it gives me hope that new generations of kids still see Kurt Cobain as a mile marker to their growth. Those words, the moodiness of the music—it's not dated. It only gets better with time. In a world of sell-outs, they never did. They're not in soap commercials or selling Nikes to assholes. Nirvana is still pure. I honor Kurt's memory by remembering he was the one to tell me I wasn't alone, even when he was gone. A scared kid who'd just lost the woman who took him to buy *In Utero* for his birthday needed that.

EXISTENTIAL THIRST TRAP

That's why I love Nirvana and I love Kurt Cobain. He was many things, and now, he's an icon, but he's still managed to do something after death: remain with me, for me, forever. To this day, I compound his suicide and my grandmother's death as the same loss. Both of their memories are interconnected. Everything I saw, felt, and experienced was internalized, processed through a childhood rage that didn't manifest in ways that were destructive but bled out through what I consumed.

I'd already been a kid into rock and roll, metal, grunge, punk, but because no other music captured that spirit, the tangibility for emotion, there was no going back. The sound of a guitar cranked to the ceiling with booming drums and a singer wailing their hearts out became the lynchpin to my emotional process.

Twenty-three years after Kurt's passing, all those feelings came up again when Chris Cornell died. That one hurt too. Cornell felt like a mile-marker for that time, for my generation. I had a front row seat to his rise and watched the band become a part of the cultural lexicon. Once again, I had to process the death of a stranger everyone seemed to know. I shared my grief, with a sense of ownership in relationship to my life and personal experience with that person. Soundgarden's music was a part of my childhood and remains a part of me as a growing human. There's poetry in those phrases; they stick with me, imprinting my bones with an aloof suffering. I don't think that was on purpose. It's just symptomatic of the generation. There's always a little tinge of suffering for Gen-X that's inescapable, no matter how happy someone may be.

Losing Layne from Alice in Chains or Scott Weiland from Stone Temple Pilots was, sadly, not surprising. I wanted them to get better, to regain their forms as musicians, idols, and icons. But that would never come to pass. In comparison, Chris Cornell's suicide was unexpected. He didn't waste away before my eyes, drained by addiction, AIDS, or other diseases. He didn't go out in a flame of glory or lose his life to a fluke accident. Frankly, I thought he was the one who was most likely to make it. He seemed like he had a chance.

I mourned him because he was someone I considered to be keeping the flame of rock and roll alive. Despite being elder statesmen in the game, Soundgarden is a meat and potatoes band. They make the kind of music that everyone can carry in their pocket but feels uniquely "theirs." For a lot of people, the songs we love are psychological footnotes in our greater story. Soundgarden carries that weight for me.

They *were* and *are* different. They're a band who crossed the lines of so many styles and categories. Those riffs are powerhouses, sludgy masterpieces. From the vocal range to the destructive, bombastic drums, or the in the shadows but totally amazing bass playing, Soundgarden was a band of pure players. They'd dabble in metal here and there or define a notion of grunge; I may be mistaken, but I think one song might have some banjo. There's an inescapable presence in their music that feels timeless. I think the word for it is *soul*.

One memory, though, it sticks out anytime I think of Soundgarden. I remember they'd dropped *Superunknown,* and the world was at their feet in the wave of "Black Hole Sun." While I saved my pennies to buy a cassette, some of my friends weren't so keen. Soundgarden was too whiny for them, not hard enough. Fine. I remember playing the cassette for a Mexican friend whose world was hip hop while mine was rock and roll. We did a music exchange, with him showing me Warren G and Nate Dogg's *Regulators* and me showing him Soundgarden. It was a brilliant afternoon. Maybe this seems small, but I remember that time as uniquely innocent. Back then, things like the music you liked didn't define your

EXISTENTIAL THIRST TRAP

friendship. The barriers of identity that cropped up later in life weren't up yet, and we hadn't become guarded like so many do. To this day, I'm a nerd. I obsess about music, about records, about every aspect of the artform. I connect with people who feel the same.

In this memory, the music swap was pure. We each took something from the other and accepted it. We defined that summer by trading my grunge or punk or metal for hip hop. I now liked Snoop Dog or Cypress Hill, and he now liked Metallica or Nirvana. But, before those tracks, I remember it was Soundgarden that opened that door. I grew as a person because of one song and one summer. The grunge lyrics I committed to memory like scripture are still part of me today, and when I find someone else who loves those albums like I do, it's like meeting someone from a country we both left long ago, someone who speaks my language and can get down to the same groove. It may seem insignificant for most, but I like to remember those pure moments, the ones that exist on the axis of absolute joy. Now, so many years later, I still do.

I HOPE THERE ARE CROCODILES IN HEAVEN

I MISS THE Crocodile Hunter and the honesty, wholesomeness, and integrity of Steve Irwin. There's an old George Carlin bit where he talks about praying to Joe Pesci rather than the Christian God because Joe Pesci gets shit done. In the same way, I look to Steve Irwin as my moral compass. There's never a sketchy story about him. There's no "Dark Side of Australia Zoo." Instead, it's all khaki shorts, mullets, and life lessons. The guy has been dead for over a decade now, and his words still warm my dead, black soul.

Where I live, if someone gives you a hug, it's from the heart.

Some of my poor choices would have offended the Crocodile Hunter. I look back on the time when I was shitfaced and blowing fireballs outside of bars in the French Quarter while Steve Irwin was calling snakes trying to rip his lips off "beauties." We are not made of the same material. While I've laid in bed till 3 p.m. fighting off a hangover, this man was out there making sure people knew that *crocodiles* should be loved and respected.

I have no fear of losing my life. If I have to save a koala or a crocodile or a kangaroo or a snake, mate, I will save it.

When Steve Irwin died, I was legitimately sad. I've gotten emotional only a handful of times when someone passes on to the next realm. Losing this legend to a fucking stingray sucked. If only he'd left the damn barb in there. We'd still have him. This dude taught an entire generation of kids in the 90s to appreciate nature no matter what animal it was. He taught us to look at each animal like it was the best thing we could ever encounter, from bugs to bats.

"I believe that education is all about being excited about something," he told the *Scientific American* in 2001. "Seeing passion and enthusiasm helps push an educational message."

There are worse people to think about when everything sucks. Because life is a big bag of ass, and once you accept that it's going to suck, it makes navigating through the noise a lot easier (well, this is what Buddhism teaches me). I looked up to Steve, who never got mad if some monitor lizard would snack on his arm or some shit. He wouldn't get crazy. He understood it was their way and they were acting on instinct, this creature taken out of the wild. If only more of us could look at life with a lens like that—that we're moving across nature's landscape, that not everything is a carnal husk to suck the marrow clean out. We'd probably live in a much more peaceful and verdant world. But here we are. And you know what? I don't know if it's possible to live up to Steve, but I don't mind giving it a try.

I'm not the only fan out there, and that makes the world seem like a friendlier place too. They named a snail after the guy. It's called "Crikey Steve Irwini." I'm glad we have something to remember him by. The man who pulled koalas out of burning trees got a statue and a slimy yellow shelled land mollusk in his honor. That seems fitting. I don't think he'd mind a bit.

Steve Irwin taught me that learning about animals is one of the best ways to learn about ourselves. This is why I like zoos. Now, zoos are a topic of some debate. Some folks believe it's intrusive to the animal's life to keep it in captivity, while others stand by that giving people the chance to see and interact with animals is an excellent way to bring conservation efforts toward the fore. I'm in the second group. If I've got a few hours to kill in any city, you'd best believe I wanna see their reptile house. I find a sense of calm roaming through the enclosures, seeing the hippos float around in their moat, or when the lion lets a massive roar loose to make sure everyone knows who's in charge. During the New Orleans chapter of my life, I'd hit Audubon Zoo to see the Komodo dragons roam their glass pit. I love passing the pool of flamingos, jealous that all they cared about was eating and not falling over despite standing on one leg. I needed the peace of seeing the tigers roam their square footage of ground. There was something special, exploring the African savannah like this—complete with music pumped in over the speakers. My daily life was schlepping beers to tourists on Bourbon Street while dealing with drunks, vomit-stained shoes, and a need for peace that no bottle of beer could provide. The zoo offered a serenity that grounded me.

When I lived in Chicago, hitting Lincoln Park Zoo was one of my favorite things to do, no matter the season. Because it's free and open every day of the year, that zoo was a great way to process getting fired from a job, losing a girlfriend, and, later on, knowing that my marriage was over. There's a purity about the place. I saw a simpler version of myself behind the bars, wallowing in the ponds, and lounging in the grass. The zoo was a place where I could shed our world and engage with the primitive. Observing these creatures seems to act as a glue that binds deeper than our cultures and toxic tribalism. We can argue about the best burrito in town, but most will come together over watching otters play because that shit is cute.

I've walked the winding miles past elephants, strolled past the bored kangaroos. I'll always make a stop in my

EXISTENTIAL THIRST TRAP

beloved Australia house. Sharing their space, feeling their innocent energy, makes me whole when humanity loves to chew at the core of who I am daily.

When we were kids, we'd take field trips to both Lincoln Park and Brookfield Zoos. While both have their merits, I always enjoyed Lincoln Park most. The gorilla house was small back in the day. And the silverbacks would sometimes beat on the glass, giving me the scare of a lifetime. That was always a better thrill than what I got up to later in life—walking around, listening to Tyler Childers, sad that my wife probably didn't love me anymore.

I loved going on a winter day. All of the animals were active because it wasn't so hot. No one would be there. I drifted in and out of the exhibits listening to Portishead or Bjork (no matter where I am, I'm forever a sad person). That zoo was one of many that offered a serenity that grounded me. I've been to the Atlanta Zoo and every zoo in Texas. I loved seeing Taronga Zoo in Sydney, but Lincoln Park Zoo will always be a spiritual spot for me. I love the way the penguin house smells. Watching keepers feed the animals, that's my kind of Zen. It's not a show but a moment of peace.

Back in my early 20s, friends and I went to Brookfield Zoo in Chicago. We walked past the vultures snacking on some carrion. We stopped at Baboon Island, where the primates were marooned on this big rock. The word on the street was once this population of baboons died out, they wouldn't be breeding anymore.

The baboons were too much for an enclosure; they were too violent. As we watched them fight one another, one of my friends laughed and pointed at one of them. They locked eyes. The baboon threatened him, showing his teeth. Even twenty feet away, we all jumped when he lunged in our direction.

While we thought it was funny then, there was a lot to take away from that experience: if we could just shut the fuck up and enjoy the gifts around us, they'll teach us things. Every lesson is a good thing, even if it means losing an eyeball to a pissed off primate.

My love of zoos and exotic animals went to the next level a few years ago when I got an opportunity to visit the Southern Hemisphere in person. I had convinced a major tech company that I should write for them. Not bad for a kid who moved to New Orleans with $300 in his pocket. Only a couple years before, I'd been dancing for dollars on Bourbon Street stages to T Pain songs on Christmas Eve.

This tech company was headquartered in Sydney. They made it a point to make Australian culture a part of the company's culture, which meant they were pretty cool about people visiting HQ if you had a "business reason." Naturally, I put the business case together—it was complete bullshit—and fooled them not once but *twice* into paying my way to the Land Down Under. I couldn't believe this. It was an all-time, bucket list, greatest hits trip.

On the short list of things I lose my shit over, Australia is one of them. I am a fan of the highest order. I've got their states memorized. I sprang for a Steve Irwin Funko, which gazes at me while I work. I can name Prime Ministers and even know the capital (Canberra). I'll drop random-ass facts on you about Australia's treatment of its indigenous people or that they have penguins specific to the island. I'm an Aussie trivia vending machine. I also love koalas, though I'd only ever seen them through glass or on YouTube. Australia, which is like one massive open-air zoo, was a literal dream come true.

Once I arrived in Sydney, I hit the streets every morning fresh as a goddamn golden wattle (Australia's national flower). I made new friends, saw homies I knew from the power of the Internet, and discovered this rad little bar called Spooning Goats, where I got shithammered every other night. I lived at the regional fast-food chain Oporto and hit every used bookstore in town. I bought

EXISTENTIAL THIRST TRAP

first-press UK vinyl of Nirvana's *Nevermind* and *In Utero* off a guy under a tent on a street corner, two records I'll never sell.

I took trains and buses for hours to see koalas at Featherdale Wildlife Park on my first trip. For the record, koalas smell like cough drops and their fur is filthy, like a street dog. They're also stoned to the gills on eucalyptus. I got a picture with one—tragically, I was wearing a fedora, so I'm not able to share it with anyone.

Bad fashion choices aside, Australia was all I imagined and more. I saw the coastal waters crash against the beach. I took the ferry to Taronga Zoo, which felt like making a pilgrimage to Jurassic Park. This zoo was unlike any other I'd ever been to. I walked with gray kangaroos, and I saw the Tasmanian devils snapping and growling at one another. I was there for one particular animal—my favorite, the platypus. Platypuses typically die within a month in captivity. There are, like, three zoos in the entire world that have them. And they're nocturnal, so the chance of me seeing one in the first place was rare, considering it was around 9 a.m.

Nevertheless, I went. The platypus enclosure was a small, quiet, dark room. I hung at the tank. Waiting, waiting. People came and went. They gave up quickly, bored that the animal didn't come out after a few minutes. Not me. I had flown halfway around the world for this, and I wasn't going to give up the opportunity.

I waited for her to emerge from her cave. As I listened to music, I began to feel that there was more to this than just seeing a marsupial in a cage. It felt like a pilgrimage. I sensed that the platypus would heal me in some way, that she had the power to let me know I had the ability to press on, no matter how fragile life was. I waited and refused to budge. Thirty minutes passed. My legs ached, so I walked outside to stretch in the vicious sun. A couple of feet down the stone walkway, I saw a wooden cut-out of the animal, as though taunting me. *You're giving up now?* I turned around and went back inside, resolved that I'd wait another hour if I had to.

I'm glad I did. After about five minutes, I saw something stir. She was hiding in a little smoked-glass box. She popped out in one smooth movement and glided into the water. My heart leaped with her. She was smaller than I'd imagined. As she dug for shrimp in the bed of rocks, I was entranced. She made a few laps around her tank, and I made peace with my screwups. I watched her roll through the water—sleek, innocent, and purposeful. I gave my jumping heart to a little complicated creature, something that felt like me. It was a moment I will never forget.

The next day, I started even earlier than I had before. I walked from my hotel in Newtown all the way to downtown Sydney to the Royal Botanical Gardens. The interior was a lush canopy of flowers and trees. The greens were so verdant, it felt like I was lost in an ethereal place not of this earth. Cockatiels, flying foxes, and lizards squeaked and squawked. Folks jogged past me while I drank it all in. I was keenly aware that when my lights went out, this would be on the highlight reel. I was determined to give my dying self the best show on Earth. With a flat white in hand, I grabbed a seat at Miss Macquarie's Chair, an enclave of rocks that looked out toward Sydney Harbor, the famed Opera House sitting just to the left.

The trip was also a chance to hang with my friend Andrew. He's an Aussie, half-Japanese with an immigrant mother, so he's got the legit food spots down.

While the nationalized cuisine is *suspect* outside of meat pies, steak, and chicken schnitzel, the Asian food scene in Sydney is insane. We grabbed laksa, which is a soup that's light years better than ramen. The umami broth is Nicki Minaj-thick, and there's a ton of spice, coconut, and lemongrass. On one of my last days on my last trip, Andrew hit me up for an early dinner, swearing he had the

EXISTENTIAL THIRST TRAP

hook up on a place so authentic, there weren't even menus in English. He called it the *best in town*. I was all about it.

The restaurant was in a weird part of Sydney, in one of the odd underground malls. I passed clusters of supermarkets and food courts and high-end stores, hung a right and went up the stairs, and next thing I knew, I was lost in a tiny neighborhood where the signs were in Chinese and Malaysian. Andrew and I sat down in this small Vietnamese-Chinese restaurant. He ordered cold chicken, and I asked for pho.

When our food arrived, he got cold—I mean *gelatinous*, from-the-fridge—chicken chunks of every variety sitting on a pile of warm rice. Tasting it, I was not prepared for the flavor and texture combination. It did not feel like the good ole chicken fried rice like I get in Austin's China Cafe. Digging into my bowl of pho, it smelled amazing. I slurped the broth, pulling out wads of noodles with my chopsticks.

"I've never had something like this before," I commented as I shoveled something I didn't recognize down my gullet.

Looking down at my bowl, he laughed at me. "Ah, you had a bit of liver, mate."

Dangling between my chopsticks was the liver of some animal. I had no idea. Dropping the gray matter back into the broth, I dug around, pulling out tripe, kidney, and other offal. It was authentic, all right—and my American palate was not designed to accommodate it. Andrew went back to work on his chicken and rice like a professional, while I pushed my bowl politely aside, accepting that the universe had humbled this idiot tourist once again. I realized that the "Asian food" I was used to was tame in comparison with this perfectly seasoned Vietnamese dish. I was used to strip-mall-quality orange chicken and a bunch of other Americanized stuff that they wouldn't serve on the mainland. I wanted to finish my meal, but I couldn't make myself do it.

Later, I ended up grabbing a double Bondi burger at Oporto with my tail tucked between my legs. I was grateful to have one more meal with a friend in a place I'd have never walked into randomly, supporting these warm people whose food they wanted to share. To say it was memorable was an understatement.

In the end, of course, the corporate job figured out what I'd known all along—I didn't fit in, and no matter what I tried, I was shortly out of a gig. I wouldn't say it was a wash. The visit to Sydney was one I had dreamt about as a child. I'd met talented people. I got to hug a koala. And I got to be a little closer to the best man I know—Australia's favorite son, Steve Robert Irwin. Walking under the same sun, on the same land, admiring and experiencing the same animals he grew up with made me feel like some part of me was good that way too. Even on my worst days, I like to think a little platypus swims in my heart—weird, sweet, rare, and worth waiting for.

ACKNOWLEDGMENTS

This book would not exist without the help of a lot of people. Shout out to Claire Rudy Foster for being my everything and editor. Jacob Knabb for the eternal wisdom. Brandon Lewin and the Big Laugh Comedy crew for believing in me and that books could be a part of the company's vision.

Other vital people and beta readers in this frankensteined process: Lauren Jacobs, John Baltisberger, Max Booth, Lori Michelle, Mike Precheur, Marty Shambles, Nick Gaudio, Ashton Curtis, Mika Spence, Alina Sturgess, Matt Slayer, Matthew Revert, Justin Adame, and Brian Bochenek. Extra special shout out to Sarah Sudlow; even though we're divorced, you're still wildly important to me.

I would also like to thank Glenn Danzing for writing "We Are 138."

ABOUT THE AUTHOR

Robert Dean is a journalist, raconteur, and enlightened dumbass. His work has been featured in places like *MIC, Eater, Fatherly, Yahoo, Austin American-Statesman, Consequence of Sound, Ozy, USA Today,* to name a few. He's appeared on CNN and NPR. He also serves as features writer for *Hussy Magazine, Culture Clash, Pepper Magazine,* and is editor in chief for Big Laugh Comedy, Texas' premier comedy production company. He lives in Austin and loves ice cream and koalas.

CPSIA information can be obtained
at www.ICGtesting.com
Printed in the USA
JSHW081400160223
37578JS00004B/9